GMAT Practice Questions

Sentence Correction

GMAT Free
www.GMATFree.com

CONTENTS

INTRODUCTION

This book includes practice in Sentence Correction, one of the three question types on the Verbal section of the GMAT.

Improvement in Sentence Correction, of all GMAT question types, depends most critically on practice with realistic questions. The test maker does not list required knowledge for Sentence Correction, grammatical or other, so the required knowledge must be inferred from questions and learned through practice. Making matters worse, many GMAT prep providers, in an attempt to appear comprehensive, have padded their materials with grammar rules and vocabulary that will give you no advantage on the exam. Simultaneously, they typically pass over the essential insight required for success, which is that Sentence Correction only partially tests grammar knowledge and often hinges entirely on identifying and expressing the intended meaning of a sentence.

In these pages, you can count on realistic practice. Each question in this volume has been benchmarked against a real GMAT question in its format, difficulty, subject matter, and concepts tested. And the explanations are tracked against not elaborate methods, but rather realistic, expert approaches that you can absorb and adopt.

Your guide in this review is Andrew Mitchell, Chief Freedom Officer of GMAT Free LLC, the former Director of GMAT Programs at Kaplan Test Prep, dubbed the "Guru of the GMAT" by Poets & Quants, and cited as a GMAT expert by publications including *The Wall Street Journal*, *The New York Times* and *Bloomberg BusinessWeek*.

While books can be a more convenient (and relaxing) way to practice, it's important to practice occasionally on a computer screen, for the sake of realism. You can do that at the free GMAT prep course we offer at www.gmatfree.com—registration is optional.

Thank you for your purchase. Let's get going!

>> Download the free
SC Strategy Sheets
GMATFree.com/SC-Strategy-Sheets

THE SENTENCE CORRECTION STRATEGY

Step 1: Create a "filter" and apply it to evaluate the answer choices. Attempt to identify at least defect the original sentence and before you turn to the answer choices. If you find no defect, you can choose a tentative filter or skip to Step 2.

There are two **universal tests** that can be applied to every Sentence Correction question:

- **Correctly formed independent clause.** Every sentence must have at least one subject-verb pair, so you can check every question for subject-verb agreement and for the use of the proper verb tense.
- **Proper expression of intended meaning.** The original sentence in every question has an intended meaning, which is obvious from context or can be inferred from contextual clues. Check whether the grammar of the sentence conveys the intended meaning.

The following are **conditional tests,** which you should apply given a matching condition:

- **Pronouns.** Pronouns must have a clear reference, and they must match what they stand for in number (singular vs. plural).
- **Comparisons** must be phrased so that they compare logically comparable things according to the intended meaning of the sentence.
- **Parallelism:** lists, comparisons, and two-part constructions (such as "either... or...") must consist of items in the same grammatical form (e.g., all infinitives, or all simple past tense verbs).
- **Modifiers,** including as adverbs and modifying phrases, should be near what they modify.
- Certain **idioms,** which are not subject to any general rule and can be memorized only individually, must be used properly.

Step 2: Identify objective defects. Identify points of difference in the answer choices and eliminate answer choices based on those differences.

- How it's applied:
    - If you were convinced in Step 1 that the sentence is correct as written, then you can skip directly to this step, beginning with answer choice (B).
    - If any answer choices remain after you have attempted to create and apply a filter, you can use this method to finish answering the question.
    - If you eliminated all answer choices except one in Step 1, you can skip this step or use it to confirm your answer, depending on how you're doing on time on the Verbal section.
- First, look for differences based on the conditional tests described above. If you have difficulty deciding between two answer choices:
    - Look for another point of difference between them that may be easier to evaluate objectively – the answer choices often differ in more than one respect.
    - Focus on elimination – on ruling answer choices out until only one remains, rather than ruling one answer choices in.
    - Use your ear only when you can't identify an objective defect.

SENTENCE CORRECTION PRACTICE QUESTIONS

Of all the classic silent films that preceded the advent of movies with sound, <u>maybe none was more influential as</u> Metropolis, the 1927 film by Fritz Lang set in a futuristic urban dystopia.

- ○ maybe none was more influential as
- ○ it may be that none was more influential as
- ○ perhaps it is none that was more influential than
- ○ maybe it is none that was more influential than
- ○ perhaps none was more influential than

Classic Silent Film

Of all the classic silent films that preceded the advent of movies with sound, <u>maybe none was more influential as</u> Metropolis, the 1927 film by Fritz Lang set in a futuristic urban dystopia.

- ○ maybe none was more influential as
- ○ it may be that none was more influential as
- ○ perhaps it is none that was more influential than
- ○ maybe it is none that was more influential than
- ○ perhaps none was more influential than

Explanation

Creating a filter: Since we're just getting started, we'll go slower on our initial approach to this question. First, we should always check the number of the subject and verb of the independent clause. These are okay: "none" is grammatically singular (usually) and "was" is grammatically singular, so they match. There is a dependent clause, and in that clause, the subject and verb match in number once again: "films" and "preceded" are both plural. Second, the tenses of the verbs make tense. We are talking about a period in the past and both verbs use the past tense; nothing more complicated is needed. Having covered the verbs, we can check for pronouns. This sentence contains none of the typical suspicious pronouns, such as "it" or "they."

At this point, we could ask ourselves whether the grammatical expression of the sentence is correctly conveying the intended meaning. But first, the sentence sounds funny, especially around the words "more influential as." This phrase using improper idiom. **The word "as" is used for comparisons that express equality; comparisons that express inequality must use the word "than."** We'll use this error to filter out incorrect answer choices.

Applying the filter: Let's check for answer choices that use the word "than." That leads us to scan the ends of the answer choices. Choices (A) and (B) are out, while (C) through (E) have a valid "more influential than."

Identifying objective defects: in the remaining choices, (C) and (D) have an odd construction "it is none," which offends my ear and has a pronoun with no clear reference, namely "it." The correct answer is (E).

Reading difficulty can be measured according to Flesch-Kincaid grade levels; <u>if they rate a passage at higher grade level, the more difficult</u> the passage is to comprehend.

○ if they rate a passage at higher grade level, the more difficult
○ rating a passage at a higher grade level, it is that much more difficult
○ the higher a passage's grade level, the more difficult
○ the higher a passage's grade level, it is that much more difficult that
○ when a passage's grade level is higher, the more difficult it is

READING LEVELS

Reading difficulty can be measured according to Flesch-Kincaid grade levels; <u>if they rate a passage at higher grade level, the more difficult</u> the passage is to comprehend.

- ○ if they rate a passage at higher grade level, the more difficult
- ○ rating a passage at a higher grade level, it is that much more difficult
- ○ the higher a passage's grade level, the more difficult
- ○ the higher a passage's grade level, it is that much more difficult that
- ○ when a passage's grade level is higher, the more difficult it is

EXPLANATION

Creating a filter: When read the sentence, we hit a flag. We have suspicious pronoun, "they." "They" is a pronoun with a vague reference. As the sentence is written, "they" refers to the Flesch-Kincaid grade levels, but that's not what the imaginary author of this sentence is trying to express. The correct answer must fix this error, so we have an expectation to apply to the answer choices as a filter.

Applying the filter: Choice (A) is the only answer choice with the "they" problem, but (B) and (D) have an "it" problem. "It," like "they," is a pronoun without a clear reference. Actually, (E) has it too, and the word "when" is also dubious, because we are not really describing something that is related to time, but rather to the logical characteristics of a passage of text that is being graded. So (C) must be right. We plug it back in. It's elegant; this is what the imaginary author of the sentence was trying to say. The correct answer is (C).

Toward the end of that year, the food and beverage entrepreneur was looking for a partner - <u>someone not only who could provide expertise in developing talent pipelines, but sharing his passion as well to launch</u> a new product on the market.

- ○ someone not only who could provide expertise in developing talent pipelines, but sharing his passion as well to launch
- ○ someone who not only could provide expertise in developing talent pipelines, but also shared his passion to launch
- ○ someone who not only could provide expertise in developing talent pipelines, but also share his passion to launch
- ○ that being someone who not only could provide expertise in developing talent pipelines, but sharing his passion for launching
- ○ being someone who not only could provide expertise in developing talent pipelines, but share his passion as well, launching

FOOD AND BEVERAGE PARTNER

Toward the end of that year, the food and beverage entrepreneur was looking for a partner - <u>someone not only who could provide expertise in developing talent pipelines, but sharing his passion as well to launch</u> a new product on the market.

- ○ someone not only who could provide expertise in developing talent pipelines, but sharing his passion as well to launch
- ○ someone who not only could provide expertise in developing talent pipelines, but also shared his passion to launch
- ○ someone who not only could provide expertise in developing talent pipelines, but also share his passion to launch
- ○ that being someone who not only could provide expertise in developing talent pipelines, but sharing his passion for launching
- ○ being someone who not only could provide expertise in developing talent pipelines, but share his passion as well, launching

EXPLANATION

Creating a filter: There are a few flags in this sentence. By "flags," we mean grammatical elements that may not be present in a sentence, but which we should immediately check when we see them. **"Not only... but also..." is a two-part expression. For all two-part expressions, we should check that the wording is parallel, in a) the sequence of the words and b) the conjugation of the two things in the construction.** Here, the verbs are not parallel: "Sharing" should be "share" to match "provide." The sentence could correctly read, "not only provide... but also share." We'll use that as our filter and go to the answer choices.

Applying the filter: our filter leaves us with only two choices, (C) and (E).

Finding objective defects: Choice (E) has other problems. It includes the word "being" unnecessarily at the beginning of the sentence. **Gerunds of the verb "to be," such as "being," are often in error, especially when they can be omitted from the sentence.** Also, where it says "launching" at the end of the phrase, it changes the meaning of the sentence. The imaginary author of this sentence is trying to talk about sharing a specific passion, a "passion to launch" something. We briefly confirm that the other answer choices are in error. The correct answer is (C).

While a wealth of data <u>support the belief that there is a recession already</u> under way, some analysts say that conclusive evidence will not be available until next quarter.

- ○ support the belief that there is a recession already
- ○ supported the belief for there being a recession already
- ○ had supported the belief for a recovery already being
- ○ supports the belief that a recession is already
- ○ supports the belief for a recession already

RECESSION UNDERWAY

While a wealth of data <u>support the belief that there is a recession already</u> under way, some analysts say that conclusive evidence will not be available until next quarter.

- ○ support the belief that there is a recession already
- ○ supported the belief for there being a recession already
- ○ had supported the belief for a recovery already being
- ○ supports the belief that a recession is already
- ○ supports the belief for a recession already

EXPLANATION

Creating a filter: When we read the sentence, we apply the brakes at "wealth of data support." We *always* check the subject and verb of a sentence, because every sentence must have a subject and verb. The subject is "wealth" and the verb is "support." That's wrong, because "wealth" is grammatically singular, even if its meaning conveys or implies plurality. We know the grammatical subject of the sentence isn't "data" because "data" is an object of the preposition "of." **A noun that is the object of a preposition cannot be the subject of a verb; when you are looking for the noun that is the subject of a particular verb, you can ignore prepositional phrases.** So, the correct answer probably has "wealth of data *supports*." Let's check the answer choices.

Applying the filter: We are down to (D) and (E).

Finding objective defectives: (D) is much better than (E). **When a sentence expresses an indirect statement — someone else's belief, assertion, or statement — it is typically introduced as a clause with the word "that."** And that's what's happening here. So the answer must be (D). We confirm that (B) and (C) are bogus. The verb tenses are off, since this belief is a general one, expressed in the present tense, and additionally they use the phrase "there being" and "already being," which are awkward. The correct answer is (D).

In a recent study published in *Nature Neuroscience*, a team of <u>scientists, concluding that since participants who took caffeine tablets outperformed participants who took placebo tablets on a memory test,</u> caffeine enhances short-term memory.

○   scientists, concluding that since participants who took caffeine tablets outperformed participants who took placebo tablets on a memory test,

○   scientists, concluding that since participants who took caffeine tablets outperformed participants who took placebo tablets on a memory test, and

○   scientists concluded that since participants who took caffeine tablets should outperform participants who took placebo tablets on a memory test,

○   scientists concluded that since participants who took caffeine tablets did outperform participants who took placebo tablets on a memory test,

○   scientists concluded that since participants who took caffeine tablets outperformed participants who took placebo tablets on a memory test,

CAFFEINE MEMORY

In a recent study published in *Nature Neuroscience*, a team of <u>scientists, concluding that since participants who took caffeine tablets outperformed participants who took placebo tablets on a memory test,</u> caffeine enhances short-term memory.

- scientists, concluding that since participants who took caffeine tablets outperformed participants who took placebo tablets on a memory test,
- scientists, concluding that since participants who took caffeine tablets outperformed participants who took placebo tablets on a memory test, and
- scientists concluded that since participants who took caffeine tablets should outperform participants who took placebo tablets on a memory test,
- scientists concluded that since participants who took caffeine tablets did outperform participants who took placebo tablets on a memory test,
- scientists concluded that since participants who took caffeine tablets outperformed participants who took placebo tablets on a memory test,

EXPLANATION

Creating a filter: On our read of the prompt, "that since" may sound a little funny. However, "that" introduces the statement that is the belief of the scientists, according to proper usage. And the statement just happens to begin with the word "since," which introduces a dependent clause. Moreover, all the answer choices have the phrase "that since." Supposing that we don't see any other error, we can move to the answer choices without a filter and search for objective defects.

Finding objective defects: All the answers are starting out the same, but we see differences at the ends of the lines of each answer choices. "And," "should," "did." **To find objective defects, we can first compare the answer choices and look for differences.**

Choice (B) is flawed because of the "and" at the end: it changes the meaning of the sentence. The scientists are drawing a conclusion in this sentence, and that conclusion is the last four words of the sentence, a clause all on its own, and since it's the sole conclusion, what precedes it is evidence for the conclusion, and it shouldn't be preceded by an "and."

Choice (C) is out, because it distorts the intended meaning by replacing a finding with an expectation or moral view indicated by "should."

Choice (D) is flawed in a similar way to (C): "did outperform" does not need a "did." The word "did" seems to imply a contrast with a prior opinion or belief, but there are no hints in the sentence of such an intended meaning.

That leaves us with choices (A) and (E), which are similar. Comparing them, we find that (A) has an error that we hadn't noticed at first. It has no main verb! The phrase starting with "concluding" is a dependent clause and can be logically extracted from the sentence, leaving "scientists caffeine enhances" and there is no verb in the sentence. So (A) is wrong; it failed to pass our first universal test, the test of the subject and verb of the independent clause. The correct answer is (E).

In 2004 poor global weather forced the company to reduce its stockpile of oil to about 1,000 barrels, about 20 percent <u>less than those of the 2003 reserves</u>.

- ○ less than those of the 2003 reserves
- ○ less than the 2003 reserves
- ○ less than 2003
- ○ fewer than 2003
- ○ fewer than that of the company's 2003 stockpile

1,000 BARRELS

In 2004 poor global weather forced the company to reduce its stockpile of oil to about 1,000 barrels, about 20 percent <u>less than those of the 2003 reserves</u>.

- ○   less than those of the 2003 reserves
- ○   less than the 2003 reserves
- ○   less than 2003
- ○   fewer than 2003
- ○   fewer than that of the company's 2003 stockpile

EXPLANATION

Creating a filter: When we read the prompt, we find two flags in the underlined portion, the pronoun "those," and also a comparison, which contains the pronoun. The vague pronoun is muddling the comparison. Both logically and grammatically, what are we exactly comparing — barrels, years, or reserves? Or stockpiles? It can only be one. We have a filter, so we look for an answer choice to dispel this concern.

Applying the filter: Choices (C) and (D) are both simple and thus tempting. But they compare "1,000 barrels" with a *year*, 2003. We can't compare barrels with a year. Look for more objective problems, we see that choice (E) says "fewer than that." What is "that" compared to? It can't be "barrels," because that's plural, and it can't be "stockpile," because (E) mentions a stockpile later. So (E) has a bad reference and is out. We want to get rid of (A) now. The imaginary author is trying to say that the stockpile becomes 20 percent smaller. The stockpile became 1,000 barrels, according to the sentence. And the words "stockpile" and "reserves" are synonymous; they can be compared. That means (B) is okay. And, finally, we can see a defect in choice (A): the word "those," being plural, would have to refer to "barrels," but then we would have to use "fewer," not "less," since barrels are countable items. **The comparison word "fewer" must be used with countable items and the word "less" with non-countable quantities.** The correct answer is (B).

Pharmaceuticals, despite facing an ongoing innovation challenge, <u>ranks as one of the most profitable industries in a recent study, surpassed only</u> by internet and network services.

○   ranks as one of the most profitable industries in a recent study, surpassed only
○   rank as one of the most profitable industries in a recent study, only surpassed
○   has the rank of the most profitable industries in a recent study, only surpassed
○   are one of the most profitable industries in a recent study, surpassed only
○   have been ranked as one of the most profitable industries in a recent study, only surpassed

PHARMA PROFITS

Pharmaceuticals, despite facing an ongoing innovation challenge, <u>ranks as one of the most profitable industries in a recent study, surpassed only</u> by internet and network services.

- ○ ranks as one of the most profitable industries in a recent study, surpassed only
- ○ rank as one of the most profitable industries in a recent study, only surpassed
- ○ has the rank of the most profitable industries in a recent study, only surpassed
- ○ are one of the most profitable industries in a recent study, surpassed only
- ○ have been ranked as one of the most profitable industries in a recent study, only surpassed

EXPLANATION

Creating a filter: In our universal test of subject and verb, we have "pharmaceuticals" and "ranks," which are respectively the subject and verb of the sentence. "Ranks" is grammatically singular. Is "pharmaceuticals" grammatically singular or plural? The imaginary author of this sentence is talking about an industry, which is "pharmaceuticals." So it's grammatically singular, contrary to its sound. That means the sentence doesn't have any obvious error as written.

Finding objective defects: We go to the answer choices with the mission of knocking out (B) through (E), in turn. Choices (B) and (D) both use grammatically plural verbs, so they are out. Choices (C) and (E) use verbs that are grammatically singular, but introduce unnecessary wordiness. **When we look for defects in the answer choices, we can start with the same universal tests we apply to the original sentence, starting with subject and verb of the main clause.** The correct answer is (A).

The bone structure of bird-hipped dinosaurs, <u>having pubic bones which point downward and toward the tail, help explain why paleontologists believe that they</u> evolved independently of other dinosaurs.

- ○ having pubic bones which point downward and toward the tail, help explain why paleontologists believe that they
- ○ having pubic bones which point downward and toward the tail, helps explain why paleontologists believe that it
- ○ with pubic bones which point downward and toward the tail, helps explain paleontologists' believing that it
- ○ with pubic bones which point downward and toward the tail, help explain paleontologists' believing that it
- ○ with pubic bones which point downward and toward the tail, helps explain why paleontologists believe that they

Bird-Hipped Dinosaurs

The bone structure of bird-hipped dinosaurs, <u>having pubic bones which point downward and toward the tail, help explain why paleontologists believe that they</u> evolved independently of other dinosaurs.

- ○ having pubic bones which point downward and toward the tail, help explain why paleontologists believe that they
- ○ having pubic bones which point downward and toward the tail, helps explain why paleontologists believe that it
- ○ with pubic bones which point downward and toward the tail, helps explain paleontologists' believing that it
- ○ with pubic bones which point downward and toward the tail, help explain paleontologists' believing that it
- ○ with pubic bones which point downward and toward the tail, helps explain why paleontologists believe that they

Explanation

Creating a filter: Here we have a sentence in which a supporting clause adds distance between the grammatical subject and grammatical verb of the main clause, making them harder for our ears to place next to each other. **When evaluating the subject and verb of the main clause, you can omit other clauses and modifying phrases from the sentence.** The grammatical subject is "structure." The word "dinosaurs" is not the grammatical subject because it's an object of the preposition "of" in the phrase "of bird-hipped dinosaurs." The grammatical verb is "help," and putting them together we have "the structure help," which is incorrect. We need a grammatically singular verb, "helps." That's our filter.

Applying the filter: (B), (C), and (E) have it, so they remain potential correct answer.

Finding objective defects: We compare these three answer choices further. Choice (C) has the garbage phrase "paleontologists believing." As we discussed in "Food and Beverage Partner," the gerund or participle construction with "-ing" is often unnecessary. Choice (E) starts with the word "with" and ends with the word "they." We can pick on either difference; the pronoun difference is easier to check. What is that pronoun intended to refer to? Bird hipped dinosaurs: *they* evolved independently of other dinosaurs. So, actually, (E) looks good, while (B) has a pronoun error. The correct answer is (E).

The Cygnus spacecraft was grounded last week ahead of its launch date <u>due to giant coronal mass ejections from the Sun, which raised radioactivity to such levels so that their avionics systems might malfunction</u> and the navigability of the ship might be compromised.

○ due to giant coronal mass ejections from the Sun, which raised radioactivity to such levels so that their avionics systems might malfunction

○ due to giant coronal mass ejections from the Sun, thereby raising radioactivity to such levels that their avionics systems might malfunction

○ because the Sun had ejected giant coronal mass, which had raised the radioactivity to levels such that its avionics systems would malfunction

○ because of coronal mass ejections from the Sun raising the radioactivity to levels so high as to lead its avionics systems to malfunction

○ because giant coronal mass ejections from the Sun had raised the radioactivity to such levels that its avionics systems might malfunction

SOLAR EJECTIONS

The Cygnus spacecraft was grounded last week ahead of its launch date <u>due to giant coronal mass ejections from the Sun, which raised radioactivity to such levels so that their avionics systems might malfunction</u> and the navigability of the ship might be compromised.

- ○ due to giant coronal mass ejections from the Sun, which raised radioactivity to such levels so that their avionics systems might malfunction
- ○ due to giant coronal mass ejections from the Sun, thereby raising radioactivity to such levels that their avionics systems might malfunction
- ○ because the Sun had ejected giant coronal mass, which had raised the radioactivity to levels such that its avionics systems would malfunction
- ○ because of coronal mass ejections from the Sun raising the radioactivity to levels so high as to lead its avionics systems to malfunction
- ○ because giant coronal mass ejections from the Sun had raised the radioactivity to such levels that its avionics systems might malfunction

EXPLANATION

Creating a filter: We read the prompt. Supposing that we try the universal checks of subject and verb, and intended meaning, and we don't find an error, we can proceed to the answer choices and evaluate them exhaustively, skipping answer choice (A) initially.

Finding objective defects: In (B), "thereby raising" sounds funny and distorts the meaning of the sentence. It makes it sound like the spacecraft raised the levels. So (B) is out.

In choice (C), the construction at the beginning sounds weird. We look for a more objective problem and find it: it says "systems *would* malfunction," which is not parallel with the following "*might* be compromised." The intended meaning is that if one happens, the other will happen. Therefore, (C) is out.

Choice (D), similarly to (C), is not parallel due to the verb "to malfunction." So it's out.

That leaves us with (E), which sounds pretty good, and (A). We try to find a more objective difference and find it in the pronouns, "*their* avionics systems" and "*its* avionics systems." The avionics systems belong to the spacecraft, which is grammatically singular, so answer choice (A) is flawed. The correct answer is (E).

Despite many peoples' impulse to go straight to the refrigerator, the best way to store an eggplant is <u>the placing of it in a vented bowl, and, with the intention to use it as soon as possible, it is kept</u> in a cool spot away from direct sunlight.

○   the placing of it in a vented bowl, and, with the intention to use it as soon as possible, it is kept

○   placing it in a vented bowl, and, with the intention to use it as soon as possible, to keep it

○   having it placed in a vented bowl, and, with the intention to use it as soon as possible, it was laid

○   to place it in a vented bowl, and, with the intention to use it as soon as possible, to keep it

○   that it is placed in a vented bowl, which, with the intention to use it as soon as possible, was kept

EGGPLANT STORAGE

Despite many peoples' impulse to go straight to the refrigerator, the best way to store an eggplant is <u>the placing of it in a vented bowl, and, with the intention to use it as soon as possible, it is kept</u> in a cool spot away from direct sunlight.

- ○ the placing of it in a vented bowl, and, with the intention to use it as soon as possible, it is kept
- ○ placing it in a vented bowl, and, with the intention to use it as soon as possible, to keep it
- ○ having it placed in a vented bowl, and, with the intention to use it as soon as possible, it was laid
- ○ to place it in a vented bowl, and, with the intention to use it as soon as possible, to keep it
- ○ that it is placed in a vented bowl, which, with the intention to use it as soon as possible, was kept

EXPLANATION

Creating a filter: We read the question and pause at the phrase "the placing of it," which sounds ridiculous. We try to finish the phrase with our own coherent English, forgetting the sentence for a moment. What is the best way to store an eggplant? It's "to place it in a bowl"... or maybe it's "placing it in a bowl." **When the original sentence includes awkward phrasing, predict a grammatically correct, natural alternative and use that as your filter.** This reduces the chances of getting trapped between answer choices which sound roughly equal. Looking for the infinitive, "to place," we go to the answer choices.

Applying the filter, we find that (B) and (D) are contenders. But choice (B) has a lack of parallelism between "placing it" and "to keep it" at the end. Choice (D) is parallel and therefore probably right.

We can confirm by looking for objective defects in (C) and (E). Choice (C) says "it was laid," so there are instances of "it" that refer variously and hence incorrectly to the eggplant and the bowl. Choice (E) uses the past tense, when we are speaking about the present tense of general advice. **General truths or maxims are best expressed in the present tense.** The correct answer is (D).

The evolutionary theory of punctuated equilibrium maintains <u>that the characteristics that are possessed by any given species developed</u> over long periods of stability interrupted by short periods of rapid change.

- ○ that the characteristics that are possessed by any given species developed
- ○ that the characteristics that have been possessed by any given species had developed
- ○ that the characteristics of any given species were possessed and have developed
- ○ the characteristics of any given species to be a possession developed
- ○ the characteristics that are possessed by any given species to have been developed

PUNCTUATED EQUILIBRIUM

The evolutionary theory of punctuated equilibrium maintains <u>that the characteristics that are possessed by any given species developed</u> over long periods of stability interrupted by short periods of rapid change.

o   that the characteristics that are possessed by any given species developed
o   that the characteristics that have been possessed by any given species had developed
o   that the characteristics of any given species were possessed and have developed
o   the characteristics of any given species to be a possession developed
o   the characteristics that are possessed by any given species to have been developed

EXPLANATION

Creating a filter: We read the prompt, and it passes the basic tests. So we move to the answer choices and will try to eliminate exhaustively, starting with (B).

Finding objective defects: Scanning, we can note that choices (A) through (C) begin one way, (D) and (E) another. Choice (D) uses an awkward "to be" construction, so we throw it out. Recall that, in the indirect statement of a belief, the best usage is usually "that," as we discussed in Recession Underway. Choice (E) has the same problem, in an even more garbled form. So we eliminate (D) and (E).

We are down to (A), (B), and (C), which differ in their verb tenses. What's the intended meaning of the sentence? It's that the development of present characteristics happened in the past. Choice (C) puts the *characteristics* in the past, so it's out. Choice (B) tries to get fancy without adding meaning. The use of "had" in "had developed" would have to refer to point before some other point in the past, but there is no such reference in the sentence to a moment in the past and a moment *before* that. **The correct usage of past perfect (past tense with "had") is to refer to a point in the past prior to another, later point in the past. If there is no such later point, the use is incorrect.** So (B) is out. The correct answer is (A).

Like the improvements to irrigation and crop rotation, fertilizers and pesticides were developed long ago but have benefited from substantial advances in the last century.

- ○ Like the improvements to irrigation and crop rotation,
- ○ As irrigation's and crop rotation's improvements,
- ○ Like those of irrigation and crop rotation,
- ○ As it is of irrigation and crop rotation,
- ○ Like irrigation and crop rotation,

FERTILIZERS AND PESTICIDES

<u>Like the improvements to irrigation and crop rotation,</u> fertilizers and pesticides were developed long ago but have benefited from substantial advances in the last century.

- ○   Like the improvements to irrigation and crop rotation,
- ○   As irrigation's and crop rotation's improvements,
- ○   Like those of irrigation and crop rotation,
- ○   As it is of irrigation and crop rotation,
- ○   Like irrigation and crop rotation,

EXPLANATION

Creating a filter: When we read the prompt, the word "like" sends up a flag. We have a comparison, and it's problematic. Grammatically, the comparison as written is between "improvements," on one hand, and "fertilizers and pesticides" on the other. An improvement is not logically comparable with a fertilizer. **The grammatical expression of a comparison must establish the comparison between things that are logically comparable.** The imaginary author of the sentence intends to compare improvements with improvements or farm techniques with farm techniques, so we look for an answer choice that does that.

Applying the filter: Choice (E) passes our test. Choice (B) has the same problem as (A), and (C) and (D) introduce pronouns that do not clearly refer to anything, "those" and "it." The correct answer is (E).

<u>When not augmented appropriately by an increase in protein intake</u>, a weight-lifting regimen may tire muscles without building strength.

○   When not augmented appropriately by an increase in protein intake
○   In the case that it is not augmented appropriately by an increase in protein intake
○   Should it not be augmented by an appropriate increase in protein intake
○   If not appropriately augmented by an increase in protein intake
○   If not augmented by an appropriate increase in protein intake

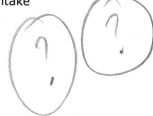

PROTEIN INTAKE

When not augmented appropriately by an increase in protein intake, a weight-lifting regimen may tire muscles without building strength.

- o When not augmented appropriately by an increase in protein intake
- o In the case that it is not augmented appropriately by an increase in protein intake
- o Should it not be augmented by an appropriate increase in protein intake
- o If not appropriately augmented by an increase in protein intake
- o If not augmented by an appropriate increase in protein intake

EXPLANATION

Creating a filter: We read the prompt, and it doesn't appear to fail the universal tests. So, we proceed to the answer choices, scanning starting with (B), to eliminate exhaustively.

Finding objective defects: upon a scan, the answer choices reveal that we are dealing with a question of how to begin this sentence. Choices (B) and (C) are hardly tempting; we have simpler ways to describe the conditional meaning of the sentence – either "if" or "when."

That leaves us with (D), (E), and maybe (A). "If" and "when" both sound natural; which is correct? Precisely, **"if" describes a condition, and "when" describes a time.** We are talking more about a conditional relationship here in the sentence that the imaginary author is attempting to compose. It's more about the conditions under which a weight-lifting regimen occurs and less about specific time periods within that regimen. On those grounds, we eliminate choice (A).

Choices (D) and (E) are identical apart from the placement of "appropriate." What is really "appropriate" here, the augmentation or the increase in protein intake? The intended meaning is that, if you lift a ton and don't increase protein a ton, that's bad. If you lift only a little, the protein intake need only be a little. It's augmented either way; what must be "appropriate" is the level of increase of protein. Therefore, "appropriate" goes near "protein," since **modifiers should be placed as near as possible to the words they modify.** The correct answer is (E).

Download the free SC Strategy Sheets at GMATFree.com/SC-Strategy-Sheets

The surge in first-quarter luxury retail and level auto <u>sales indicate that post-holiday consumer confidence is higher than analysts previously predicted</u>.

○ sales indicate that post-holiday consumer confidence is higher than analysts previously predicted
○ sales indicates that post-holiday consumer confidence is higher than analysts have previously predicted
○ sales indicates that post-holiday consumer confidence is higher as analysts have previously predicted
○ sales, indicating about post-holiday consumer confidence that it is higher than previously predicted by analysts
○ sales, indicating post-holiday consumer confidence is higher than previously predicted to be by analysts

POST-HOLIDAY CONSUMER CONFIDENCE

The surge in first-quarter luxury retail and level auto <u>sales indicate that post-holiday consumer confidence is higher than analysts previously predicted</u>.

○ sales indicate that post-holiday consumer confidence is higher than analysts previously predicted
○ sales indicates that post-holiday consumer confidence is higher than analysts have previously predicted
○ sales indicates that post-holiday consumer confidence is higher as analysts have previously predicted
○ sales, indicating about post-holiday consumer confidence that it is higher than previously predicted by analysts
○ sales, indicating post-holiday consumer confidence is higher than previously predicted to be by analysts

EXPLANATION

Creating a filter: When we read the sentence, the subject-verb agreement sounds potentially off. We cut out the prepositional phrase starting with the preposition "in," since none of the nouns in such a phrase can be the grammatical subject. That leaves "the surge indicate," which is incorrect. Choice (A) is out and we have a filter to evaluate the other choices.

Applying the filter: Choices (B) and (C) look good, according to our filter. Answer choices (D) and (E) make the sentence even worse — it no longer has a main subject and verb, as every sentence must.

Finding objective defects: We're left with (B) and (C). Choice (C) uses the comparative "higher as," which is incorrect. "Higher" is a word of unequal comparison, so, as we have discussed in Classic Silent Film, the comparison word must be "than." The correct answer is (B).

Amphibians have been able to maintain a specific level of hydration in and out of water ever since they developed neurohypophysial hormones <u>which adjusted</u> the permeability of their skin.

- which adjusted
- that adjusts
- which has adjusted
- that has been adjusting
- having adjusted

AMPHIBIAN HYDRATION

Amphibians have been able to maintain a specific level of hydration in and out of water ever since they developed neurohypophysial hormones <u>which adjusted</u> the permeability of their skin.

- ○ which adjusted
- ○ that adjusts
- ○ which has adjusted
- ○ that has been adjusting
- ○ having adjusted

EXPLANATION

Creating a filter: We read the prompt, ignoring the "neuro-" word for now. The sentence passes the subject-verb test and doesn't raise flags. We proceed to the answer choices to proceed exhaustively and eliminate choices based on objective defects.

Finding objective defects: Choice (B) has a grammatically singular verb, so it's out. Same with (C) and (D). We are referring to the grammatically plural "hormones."

So we are down to (A) and (E). Choice (E) sounds weird and is flawed. **When a clause is used to define or describe a noun, it should begin with the relative pronouns "which" or "that."** The correct answer is (A).

<u>An innovative filmmaker, Ray Harryhausen's legacy includes</u> bringing realistic dinosaurs and a variety of other gigantic, threatening creatures to the big screen.

- o   An innovative filmmaker, Ray Harryhausen's legacy includes
- o   The legacy of Ray Harryhausen, an innovative filmmaker, includes
- o   Ray Harryhausen is an innovative filmmaker including in his legacy the
- o   Included in the innovative filmmaker Ray Harryhausen's legacy are
- o   The innovative filmmaker's legacy of Ray Harryhausen includes

Ray's Legacy

<u>An innovative filmmaker, Ray Harryhausen's legacy includes</u> bringing realistic dinosaurs and a variety of other gigantic, threatening creatures to the big screen.

- ○ An innovative filmmaker, Ray Harryhausen's legacy includes
- ○ The legacy of Ray Harryhausen, an innovative filmmaker, includes
- ○ Ray Harryhausen is an innovative filmmaker including in his legacy the
- ○ Included in the innovative filmmaker Ray Harryhausen's legacy are
- ○ The innovative filmmaker's legacy of Ray Harryhausen includes

Explanation

Creating a filter: We read the prompt but don't need to go far. **When a modifying phrase begins a sentence, set off by a comma, it modifies the subject that comes after the comma, and we should check that the modification that is expressed matches the intended meaning.** As written, "an innovative filmmaker" is currently modifying "legacy." "Ray Harryhausen's" is not a noun, since it is possessive. So the sentence is expressing that a filmmaker is a legacy, which is not the intended meaning.

Applying the filter: We look for an answer choice from (B) on that resolves the modification error. All of them do! We'll have to eliminate on other grounds.

Finding objective defects: Choice (B) may be good. Choice (C) is in error because it creates the phrase "the bringing" at the end of the line and the rest of the sentence. Choice (D), similarly, creates the phrase "are bringing," and there is only a singular subject to go with "are." Choice (E) has separated "innovative filmmaker" and "Ray Harryhausen" in a nonsensical way. The correct answer is (B).

Total cloud inversion, which looks like a sea of clouds, <u>occurs about once every decade at the Grand Canyon but had been rarely captured</u> on film until recently.

○ occurs about once every decade at the Grand Canyon but had been rarely captured
○ occurs about once every decade but had rarely been captured at the Grand Canyon
○ appear about once every decade at the Grand Canyon although rarely captured
○ appear about once every decade at the Grand Canyon, although rarely having been captured
○ appear about once every decade at the Grand Canyon, which has rarely been captured

TOTAL CLOUD INVERSION

Total cloud inversion, which looks like a sea of clouds, <u>occurs about once every decade at the Grand Canyon but had been rarely captured</u> on film until recently.

o   occurs about once every decade at the Grand Canyon but had been rarely captured
o   occurs about once every decade but had rarely been captured at the Grand Canyon
o   appear about once every decade at the Grand Canyon although rarely captured
o   appear about once every decade at the Grand Canyon, although rarely having been captured
o   appear about once every decade at the Grand Canyon, which has rarely been captured

EXPLANATION

Creating a filter: In the original sentence, the verb "had been" raises a flag. As we saw in Punctuated Equilibrium, the past perfect must refer to a past point before *another* past point. That may be the intended meaning here: it had rarely been captured (=further past) until recently (=recent past). Tentatively keeping choice (A) in, we can go to the answer choices.

Finding objective defects: at a glance, the answer choices fall into two groups, the "occurs" and the "appear." We are talking about something grammatically singular, "inversion," so "occurs" is correct and "appear" is incorrect.

That leaves us with (A) and (B), which differ only in the placement of the phrase "at the Grand Canyon." One of these two options must be objectively incorrect. Which conveys the intended meaning? Choice (B) seems to say that total cloud inversion only occurs once a decade *period* — as in anywhere. We don't have to be a meteorologist to know that's probably not right: it's at the Grand Canyon that it occurs once a decade. The correct answer is (A).

Skeptics view the increase in minimum wage not as a measure that will promote the economic well-being of lower-income citizens, as it is intended to be, <u>rather as a step that will increase unemployment</u> and have the opposite of its intended effect.

o   rather as a step that will increase unemployment
o   yet as a step that will increase unemployment
o   but step that will increase unemployment
o   but as a step that will increase unemployment
o   but also as a step that may increase unemployment

MINIMUM WAGE EFFECTS

Skeptics view the increase in minimum wage not as a measure that will promote the economic well-being of lower-income citizens, as it is intended to be, <u>rather as a step that will increase unemployment</u> and have the opposite of its intended effect.

- ○ rather as a step that will increase unemployment
- ○ yet as a step that will increase unemployment
- ○ but step that will increase unemployment
- ○ but as a step that will increase unemployment
- ○ but also as a step that may increase unemployment

EXPLANATION

Creating a filter: We read the prompt. Something appears to be missing: our trained ears want to hear not only "rather," but rather "but rather." **When the word "rather" is preceded in a sentence by "not," the phrase should be "but rather," and "not [only]…but rather…" is a two-part construction requiring parallelism.** We can hear this more easily by omitting the dependent clause that starts with "that will promote…," since dependent clauses can be omitted from a sentence without impacting the grammatical of the main, independent clause. "Skeptics view the increase not as a measure that will blah blah, but rather as a step blah blah." That sounds better. We look for "but rather" in the answer choices.

Applying the filter: We don't find "but rather," but answer choice (D) solves the problem by introducing the key missing word "but," to communicate the contrast that the imaginary author of this sentence intends to convey.

Choices (C) and (E) have the word "but" but in nonsensical phrases. In choice (B), also, the word "yet" is not a proper word to convey the intended function of "but," which is to establish the proper way that the minimum wage should be viewed according to the sentence. The correct answer is (D).

Many sentence correction questions rely on knowledge of idiom; in other words, no amount of logic will help you solve them if you aren't familiar with the phrases involved. Complicating the matter is the fact that the test makers don't publish or cite any kind of list of idioms that you must know for the test. Given that, the best way to strengthen your knowledge of idioms is to go through realistic practice questions and take note of the idioms as you go. All of the practice questions in this free course are modeled after official questions released by the test maker and hence provide as good a basis of the idiomatic English knowledge you'll need for the GMAT. Again, the correct answer is (D).

Citing hard-to-predict sudden changes to the Earth's environment, a panel of advisors has urged the nation to implement an early warning system, conduct further research of threats, <u>and building a capability to respond</u> to these disruptions.

- ○ building a capability to respond
- ○ building a capability that respond
- ○ building a capability that for responding
- ○ and build a capability for responding
- ○ and build a capability to respond

CLIMATE ADVICE

Citing hard-to-predict sudden changes to the Earth's environment, a panel of advisors has urged the nation to implement an early warning system, conduct further research of threats, <u>and building a capability to respond</u> to these disruptions.

- o building a capability to respond
- o building a capability that respond
- o building a capability that for responding
- o and build a capability for responding
- o and build a capability to respond

EXPLANATION

Creating a filter: The basic structure of the sentence is that this "panel has urged the nation to A, B, and C," where A, B, and C are all verbs. **In a compound predicate – a list of verbs joined by conjunctions such as "and" – the verbs must all take on parallel form.** And they don't: "building" is not parallel with "implement" and "conduct."

Applying the filter: We look for "build" in the answer choices and narrow them down to (D) and (E).

Finding objective defects: Generally, the infinitive wins and the gerund loses, favoring (E). Furthermore, "capability for" is not a proper idiom. The correct answer is (E).

Wetlands contribute to the stability of the environment in multiple ways, preventing flooding by holding water; filtering and purifying surface water; and, surprisingly, release vegetative matter which helps feed fish in the rivers.

- ○ filtering and purifying surface water; and, surprisingly, release
- ○ filtering and purifying surface water; and, surprisingly, releasing
- ○ filtering and purifying surface water; and they surprisingly release
- ○ they filter and purify surface water; and surprisingly release
- ○ they filter and purify surface water; and, surprisingly, releasing

WETLAND FUNCTION

Wetlands contribute to the stability of the environment in multiple ways, preventing flooding by holding water; <u>filtering and purifying surface water; and, surprisingly, release</u> vegetative matter which helps feed fish in the rivers.

- ○ filtering and purifying surface water; and, surprisingly, release
- ○ filtering and purifying surface water; and, surprisingly, releasing
- ○ filtering and purifying surface water; and they surprisingly release
- ○ they filter and purify surface water; and surprisingly release
- ○ they filter and purify surface water; and, surprisingly, releasing

EXPLANATION

Creating a filter: The prompt raises a flag. Namely, we have a list, so something to check quickly is whether the elements of the list are in parallel form. By the way, there's no problem with separating the elements of a list in a sentence with semicolons, especially when some or more of the items are lengthy. This is a list of verbs, and they are "preventing," "filtering and purifying" and "release." "Release" is in error and should match the other two as "releasing." Since "preventing" is outside the underlined portion and hence can't be changed, we know that we will have to settle on "ing" forms in the correct answer.

Applying the filter: There's only one answer choice meeting our criterion. The correct answer is (B).

The number of gray whales spotted migrating south off the Southern California coast was 364 in December, prompting questions <u>whether the annual population of the endangered species possibly doubled that of</u> the 20,000 estimate of the previous year.

○ whether the annual population of the endangered species possibly doubled that of
○ whether the annual population of the endangered species was possibly double
○ of the annual population of the endangered species, that it possibly doubled
○ of the annual population of the endangered species possibly doubling that of
○ of the annual population of the endangered species, that it would possibly double that of

GRAY WHALES

The number of gray whales spotted migrating south off the Southern California coast was 364 in December, prompting questions <u>whether the annual population of the endangered species possibly doubled that of</u> the 20,000 estimate of the previous year.

- ○ whether the annual population of the endangered species possibly doubled that of
- ○ whether the annual population of the endangered species was possibly double
- ○ of the annual population of the endangered species, that it possibly doubled
- ○ of the annual population of the endangered species possibly doubling that of
- ○ of the annual population of the endangered species, that it would possibly double that of

EXPLANATION

Creating a filter: Supposing that we're not sure what to make of the prompt, or can't create a filter, we can head straight to the answer choices.

Finding objective defects: The answer choices fall into two groups, one starting with "whether" and the other starting with "of." Here, "whether" is correct, as it is the proper way to introduce a phrase that is a yes or no question. "Of" would indicate that we are questioning the animal population, which is not under cross-examination here.

That leaves us with (A) and (B). One must be objectively in error. The "that" in (A) will be either required or incorrect. What is that relative pronoun standing for? Population, apparently. That would mean, "The annual population of the species doubled the population of the 20,000 estimate of the previous year." You can't have a population of 20,000 estimate, so (A) is incorrect. The correct answer is (B).

Skunks primarily eat both plant and animal material, <u>but augmenting</u> their predatory diet by scavenging for human garbage and bird and rodent carcasses.

- ○ but augmenting
- ○ and have augmented
- ○ and even though they augment
- ○ although they augment
- ○ but with augmenting

SKUNK DIET

Skunks primarily eat both plant and animal material, <u>but augmenting</u> their predatory diet by scavenging for human garbage and bird and rodent carcasses.

- ○ but augmenting
- ○ and have augmented
- ○ and even though they augment
- ○ although they augment
- ○ but with augmenting

EXPLANATION

Creating a filter: When we read the prompt, something is off in the basic subject/verb check. The phrase after the comma makes the sentence ungrammatical. Every phrase in a sentence must be an independent clause, a dependent clause, or a modifying phrase. In this sentence, the phrase after the comma is none of those. The conjunction "but" introduces that phrase as if a subject and verb are coming to make it an independent clause, but they don't appear.

Applying the filter: Choice (D) solves the problem in that manner, with a proper conjunction, subject and verb in the words, "although they augment," respectively. Another solution would be to say simply "but augment" and lose the comma before the "but," in which case the entire sentence would be one independent clause. The correct answer is (D).

With a good development team and a dependable brand, the software giant can offer no good explanation for its operating system's <u>failed attempt to thrive, or at least gain a foothold, in a marketplace that is receptive to it</u>.

- ○ failed attempt to thrive, or at least gain a foothold, in a marketplace that is receptive to it
- ○ failing to thrive, or at least gain a foothold, in a receptive marketplace
- ○ failed attempt to thrive, or at least gain a foothold, in a receptive marketplace
- ○ failure to try and thrive, or at least gain a foothold, in a receptive marketplace
- ○ failure to thrive, or at least gain a foothold, in a receptive marketplace

OPERATING SYSTEM FAILURE

With a good development team and a dependable brand, the software giant can offer no good explanation for its operating system's <u>failed attempt to thrive, or at least gain a foothold, in a marketplace that is receptive to it</u>.

- ○ failed attempt to thrive, or at least gain a foothold, in a marketplace that is receptive to it
- ○ failing to thrive, or at least gain a foothold, in a receptive marketplace
- ○ failed attempt to thrive, or at least gain a foothold, in a receptive marketplace
- ○ failure to try and thrive, or at least gain a foothold, in a receptive marketplace
- ○ failure to thrive, or at least gain a foothold, in a receptive marketplace

EXPLANATION

Creating a filter: I read the prompt and it seems fine. On second thought, we're wary about the final word "it." What does this pronoun refer to — the software giant or the operating system? Its reference is unclear, so it's in error. We look for an answer choice that solves the pronoun problem.

Applying the filter: All of the rest do, so we will have to start over with choice (B) and look for objective defects.

Finding objective defects: The answer choices differ in how they express the failure. Choice (B) gives us "operating system's failing," which is proper grammar but poor style (i.e., awkward). In (C), "failed attempt" is somewhat redundant — failure involves an attempt. (D) and (E) are better with the simple and clear "failure." Choice (D) is out because the phrase to "try and thrive" something is colloquial English, not proper English. **The proper idiom is "try to do something," not "try *and* do something."** The correct answer is (E).

<u>As contrasted with other large mammals,</u> which tend to seek shade during the day and remain inactive, the kit fox burrows to escape the desert heat.

- ○ As contrasted with other large mammals,
- ○ In contrast to other large mammals,
- ○ Unlike the behavior of other large mammals,
- ○ Unlike that of other large mammals,
- ○ Unlike other large mammals,

The Kit Fox

<u>As contrasted with other large mammals,</u> which tend to seek shade during the day and remain inactive, the kit fox burrows to escape the desert heat.

- ○ As contrasted with other large mammals,
- ○ In contrast to other large mammals,
- ○ Unlike the behavior of other large mammals,
- ○ Unlike that of other large mammals,
- ○ Unlike other large mammals,

Explanation

Creating a filter: The original sentence has a comparison, so we should check that comparison. The answer choices here are largely similar and they all end in the word "mammals." The author's intended meaning is to contrast "mammals" with "kit fox." As for how the comparison is introduced, it's mostly idiomatic: "unlike" is correct and simple. (E) is therefore the correct answer.

Further notes: (C) and (D) both establish improper comparisons of the "kit fox" with "behavior" and "that," whatever "that" is. Therefore, the correct answer is (E). You might wonder whether "in contrast" is ever correct, since it's an English phrase, after all. I'd say that a state of contrast, for example as in the case of two colors next to each other or a setting on a TV or computer monitor, is one in which the differences between two things affects how you view both of them. We have no such thing here — only a difference, which is captured perfectly by the word "unlike." The correct answer is (E).

A team of British researchers, having spent three seasons investigating and mapping a region in West Antarctica, have discovered a massive ancient subglacial trough deeper than the Grand Canyon.

○ A team of British researchers, having spent three seasons investigating and mapping a region in West Antarctica, have

○ A team of British researchers, having investigated and mapped a region in West Antarctica over three seasons, and have

○ A team of British researchers spending three seasons investigating and mapping a region in West Antarctica, and have

○ A team of British researchers has spent three seasons investigating and mapping a region in West Antarctica,

○ A team of British researchers has spent three seasons, in a region in West Antarctica, investigating and mapping,

SUBGLACIAL TROUGH

<u>A team of British researchers, having spent three seasons investigating and mapping a region in West Antarctica, have</u> discovered a massive ancient subglacial trough deeper than the Grand Canyon.

- ○ A team of British researchers, having spent three seasons investigating and mapping a region in West Antarctica, have
- ○ A team of British researchers, having investigated and mapped a region in West Antarctica over three seasons, and have
- ○ A team of British researchers spending three seasons investigating and mapping a region in West Antarctica, and have
- ○ A team of British researchers has spent three seasons investigating and mapping a region in West Antarctica,
- ○ A team of British researchers has spent three seasons, in a region in West Antarctica, investigating and mapping,

EXPLANATION

Creating a filter: supposing that we can't find an error or create a filter, we go straight to the answer choices.

Finding objective defects: in choice (B), the words "and have" at the end makes the sentence ungrammatical. The phrase "and have" appears to refer to the team of researchers as its subject, but there is no previous verb to require the word "and." We can see this more easily to see once we ignore the modifying phrase starting with "having spent"; the word "and" is without purpose. Choice (C) has the same program as (B). Choice (D) also creates a non-sentence, leaving the verb "discovered" without a subject. Choice (E) has the same problem as (D). The correct answer is (A).

The bricks that were used in the construction of the West Virginian Georgian mansion of <u>Wappocomo were manufactured in England and used as ballast to stabilize ships loading tobacco in the James River, journeying</u> in bullock carts over the Blue Ridge Mountains and Ridge-and-Valley Appalachians.

- ○ Wappocomo were manufactured in England and used as ballast to stabilize ships loading tobacco in the James River, journeying
- ○ Wappocomo were manufactured in England and used as ballast to stabilize ships loading tobacco in the James River, journey
- ○ Wappocomo, manufactured in England and used as ballast to stabilize ships loading tobacco in the James River and journeying
- ○ Wappocomo, which had been manufactured in England and used as ballast to stabilize ships loading tobacco in the James River, and journeying
- ○ Wappocomo, which had been manufactured in England and used as ballast to stabilize ships loading tobacco in the James River, journeyed

TRAVELING BRICKS

The bricks that were used in the construction of the West Virginian Georgian mansion of <u>Wappocomo were manufactured in England and used as ballast to stabilize ships loading tobacco in the James River, journeying</u> in bullock carts over the Blue Ridge Mountains and Ridge-and-Valley Appalachians.

- ○ Wappocomo were manufactured in England and used as ballast to stabilize ships loading tobacco in the James River, journeying
- ○ Wappocomo were manufactured in England and used as ballast to stabilize ships loading tobacco in the James River, journey
- ○ Wappocomo, manufactured in England and used as ballast to stabilize ships loading tobacco in the James River and journeying
- ○ Wappocomo, which had been manufactured in England and used as ballast to stabilize ships loading tobacco in the James River, and journeying
- ○ Wappocomo, which had been manufactured in England and used as ballast to stabilize ships loading tobacco in the James River, journeyed

EXPLANATION

Creating a filter: In this question, when we read the prompt, something is off with the word "journeying." In the current expression, it introduces a phrase that modifies the bricks independently of what's in the main clause, but it's not truly independent of the manufacture in England and ship-loading in the James River. The intended meaning is that England happened first, then the use as ballast, then the overland journey. We look for an answer choice that expresses the intended meaning, specifically that chronology.

Applying the filter: Choices (B) through (D) all fail to be grammatical English sentences. In (B), "journey" has no subject. (C) and (D) have the same problem as (A) and furthermore are not proper expressions of a modifying phrase or a new clause. (E) looks good. "Had been," by using the past perfect, conveys the fact that the manufacture and ship-loading events occurred before the past tense event of "journeyed," and by omitting the dependent clause here we see that "journeyed" has a grammatical subject, which is "bricks." The correct answer is (E).

Unlike the belief of the non-academics involved that the panel proceedings are subterfuge for discrimination, the academic peers of the professor under review are better equipped to evaluate the contributions and performance of their colleague in the review of potential termination due to neglect of duty.

- ○ Unlike the belief of the non-academics involved that the panel proceedings are
- ○ Although the non-academics involved were of the belief of the panel proceedings being
- ○ Contrary to the non-academics involved believing that the panel proceedings are
- ○ Even though the non-academics involved believe that the panel proceedings are
- ○ Even with the non-academics involved believing that the panel proceedings are

PANEL SUBTERFUGE

<u>Unlike the belief of the non-academics involved that the panel proceedings are</u> subterfuge for discrimination, the academic peers of the professor under review are better equipped to evaluate the contributions and performance of their colleague in the review of potential termination due to neglect of duty.

- ○ Unlike the belief of the non-academics involved that the panel proceedings are
- ○ Although the non-academics involved were of the belief of the panel proceedings being
- ○ Contrary to the non-academics involved believing that the panel proceedings are
- ○ Even though the non-academics involved believe that the panel proceedings are
- ○ Even with the non-academics involved believing that the panel proceedings are

EXPLANATION

Creating a filter: once we get going with this prompt we see the word "unlike," so we know there's a comparison. That means that we want to confirm that the grammatical expression of comparison matches the intended meaning. It does not: stripping out the prepositional phrase starting with "of the non-academics," we see that "belief" is being compared with "peers." Since "belief" is the only of the two words in the underlined portion, that's the part that will have to change, so that we are comparing people with people. We go to the answer choices looking for this outcome.

Applying the filter: the other answer choices solve the comparison problem in (A), but they introduce other problems. In (B), "of the belief" and "proceedings being" are both questionable style. Choices (C) and (E) both have the same problem: "non-academics involved believing" is poor style — we won't give the academics an -ing verb if we can give them a pure and simple verb. That's what (D) does. The correct answer is (D).

An experimental psychology study asserts that babies who are still too young to talk and estimated <u>at as young as 9 to 10 months old are able to recognize</u> signs of friendship or animosity between adults.

- ○ at as young as 9 to 10 months old are able to recognize
- ○ as being as young as 9 to 10 months old is able to recognize
- ○ that they are as young as 9 to 10 months old have the ability to recognize
- ○ to be as young as 9 to 10 months old are able to recognize
- ○ at as young as 9 to 10 months old have recognition of

BABIES' SENSE

An experimental psychology study asserts that babies who are still too young to talk and estimated <u>at as young as 9 to 10 months old are able to recognize</u> signs of friendship or animosity between adults.

○   at as young as 9 to 10 months old are able to recognize
○   as being as young as 9 to 10 months old is able to recognize
○   that they are as young as 9 to 10 months old have the ability to recognize
○   to be as young as 9 to 10 months old are able to recognize
○   at as young as 9 to 10 months old have recognition of

EXPLANATION

Creating a filter: supposing that we can't generate a filter easily, we can move on to the answer choices (B) through (E) with the aim of finding objective defects and eliminating one by one.

Finding objective defectives: choice (B) is easily out, because it uses the singular verb "is" to refer to babies. Choice (C) is out; the word "that" is meant to introduce an indirect statement, but what follows is a run-on. (E) is clearly inferior to (A), since "have recognition of" doesn't clearly express ability, which is the point of the intended sentence. That leaves us with (A) and (D). Are the babies estimated "to be" 9 months old or estimated "at" 9 months old? We are down to an idiom, and the correct idiom here is "to be," so the answer is (D). **The word "estimated" is followed by the phrase "to be" to indicate that one thing has been estimated equal to another.** The phrase "to be" will not be correct everywhere. For example, if the verb were "considered," we would not need any words in the middle at all, we could say "the babies were considered 9 months old" (though the meaning of that sentence is odd), not "to be 9 months old." The correct answer is (D).

<u>Because surveys revealed that the airline merger had confused public perceptions of the two brands</u>, executives at the acquiring company announced that it would rename the regional carrier it had acquired.

○ Because surveys revealed that the airline merger had confused public perceptions of the two brands

○ Because of confused public perceptions of the two brands, which had been revealed by surveys to be due to the airline merger,

○ Because public perceptions of the two brands from the airline merger have been confused, as revealed by a survey,

○ Due to confused public perceptions of the two brands from the airline merger, per a survey,

○ Due to the airline merger, with the result that surveys revealed the airline merger had confused public perceptions,

Two Brands

<u>Because surveys revealed that the airline merger had confused public perceptions of the two brands</u>, executives at the acquiring company announced that it would rename the regional carrier it had acquired.

- ○ Because surveys revealed that the airline merger had confused public perceptions of the two brands
- ○ Because of confused public perceptions of the two brands, which had been revealed by surveys to be due to the airline merger,
- ○ Because public perceptions of the two brands from the airline merger have been confused, as revealed by a survey,
- ○ Due to confused public perceptions of the two brands from the airline merger, per a survey,
- ○ Due to the airline merger, with the result that surveys revealed the airline merger had confused public perceptions,

Explanation

Creating a filter: choice (A) sounds good, so we can move to eliminate the other answer choices.

Finding objective defects: choice (C) uses passive voice without need. Choices (B), (D), (E) all use "because of" and "due to." **The phrases "because of" and "due to" both end with prepositions, so they properly introduce single nouns, not clauses.** And we are dealing with a full clause here. The correct answer is (A).

In the famous thought experiment that inspired the theory of relativity, Einstein asked himself whether a beam of light would look the same to an observer moving alongside the beam at the same <u>speed as an observer</u> who was stationary.

- ○ speed as an observer
- ○ speed as to an observer
- ○ speed; just as it would to an observer
- ○ speed, as it would to an observer
- ○ speed; just as to the observer

EINSTEIN'S EXPERIMENT

In the famous thought experiment that inspired the theory of relativity, Einstein asked himself whether a beam of light would look the same to an observer moving alongside the beam at the same <u>speed as an observer</u> who was stationary.

- ○ speed as an observer
- ○ speed as to an observer
- ○ speed; just as it would to an observer
- ○ speed, as it would to an observer
- ○ speed; just as to the observer

EXPLANATION

Creating a filter: In this question, we don't have to know Einstein's physics to answer correctly, but we do need a sense of the sentence's intended meaning. People go astray on the GMAT all the time by trying to apply pure grammar and style rules without considering the intended meaning of the sentence. We are primarily comparing how light looks to a moving person and how it looks to a stationary person. Grammatically, we can extract the modifying phrase "moving alongside the beam at the same speed" without altering the surrounding grammar of the sentence. That leaves "would look the same to an observer... as an observer who was stationary." That doesn't sound terrible, but it's not a parallel comparison.

Applying the filter: choice (B) gives a parallel comparison.

Further notes: choice (A) is also ambiguous. It could also be taken to mean "would look the same to an observer.... as an observer who was stationary *would look*." Totally different meaning. (C), (D), and (E) all variously include unnecessary punctuation, repetition of the pronoun, and the word "just."

The correct answer is (B).

Weighing in on the controversial subject, the President announced that the potential construction of a new pipeline depends on <u>if it will exacerbate the problem of carbon pollution and have</u> a net effect that serves the national interest.

- ○ if it will exacerbate the problem of carbon pollution and have
- ○ whether it will exacerbate the problem of carbon pollution and have
- ○ whether or not it is likely to exacerbate the problem of carbon pollution and will have
- ○ its likelihood for exacerbating the problem of carbon pollution and having
- ○ the likelihood for it to exacerbate the problem of carbon pollution and have

PRESIDENTIAL PIPELINE

Weighing in on the controversial subject, the President announced that the potential construction of a new pipeline depends on <u>if it will exacerbate the problem of carbon pollution and have</u> a net effect that serves the national interest.

- ○ if it will exacerbate the problem of carbon pollution and have
- ○ whether it will exacerbate the problem of carbon pollution and have
- ○ whether or not it is likely to exacerbate the problem of carbon pollution and will have
- ○ its likelihood for exacerbating the problem of carbon pollution and having
- ○ the likelihood for it to exacerbate the problem of carbon pollution and have

EXPLANATION

Creating a filter: In this question, the sentence needs "whether," not "if." Here exact English differs from common English. If it's a yes or no question expressed by a clause, the proper word is always "whether." The word "if" has a different function, which is to identify a condition for something. A simple test is to use "or not" — if "or not" fits in the sentence, then the right word is "whether." I.e., "the construction of a new pipeline depends on whether *or not* it will exacerbate the problem..." makes sense, so the word must be "whether."

Applying the filter: the filter leaves us with (B) and (C). Choice (C) has multiple errors. The phrase "it is likely" is unnecessary and "will have" is not parallel or consistent with "likely to exacerbate." (D) and (E) are wordy and imprecise. "How likely" would be a viable option here, but it doesn't appear. The correct answer is (B).

Born in Portsmouth, England, Charles Dickens, often regarded as the greatest novelist of the Victorian period, worked in a blacking factory at the age of <u>12, became a journalist as a young adult, and in 1842 published a travelogue about the United States after he had visited</u> that country for the first time.

- ○ 12, became a journalist as a young adult, and in 1842 published a travelogue about the United States after he had visited
- ○ 12, became a journalist as a young adult, while publishing a travelogue in 1842 about the United States after he had visited
- ○ 12 and became a journalist as a young adult, and in 1842 published a travelogue about the United States, visiting
- ○ 12, journalist as a young adult, and in 1842 published a travelogue about the United States after he visited
- ○ 12, having been a journalist as a young adult and published in 1842 a travelogue about the United States, having visited

CHARLES DICKENS

Born in Portsmouth, England, Charles Dickens, often regarded as the greatest novelist of the Victorian period, worked in a blacking factory at the age of <u>12, became a journalist as a young adult, and in 1842 published a travelogue about the United States after he had visited</u> that country for the first time.

- o   12, became a journalist as a young adult, and in 1842 published a travelogue about the United States after he had visited
- o   12, became a journalist as a young adult, while publishing a travelogue in 1842 about the United States after he had visited
- o   12 and became a journalist as a young adult, and in 1842 published a travelogue about the United States, visiting
- o   12, journalist as a young adult, and in 1842 published a travelogue about the United States after he visited
- o   12, having been a journalist as a young adult and published in 1842 a travelogue about the United States, having visited

EXPLANATION

Creating a filter: When we read the prompt, we're seeing a list of verbs. Dickens "worked," he "became", and he "published." It looks good, so we will review the other answer choices in order to eliminate them.

Finding objective defects: in (B), the "while" does not fit with the intended meaning. He didn't publish the travelogue simultaneously with any of the other actions in the sentence, accorded to the intended meaning. Choice (C) has similar logical problems and also creates a run-on sentence because it eliminates the list structure and doesn't introduce a new subject for "published." Choice (D) has a disembodied phrase, "journalist as a young adult," which is neither a properly formed list item nor a properly formed modifier of anything. (E) indicates that he worked as a journalist and published the travelogue in 1842 prior to being 12. The correct answer is (A).

To popularize the asteroid theory of dinosaur extinction, paleontologists <u>have to provide somewhat stronger evidence than now linking</u> the disappearance of fossil records and the layer of sediment in the Earth's crust caused by an asteroid impact.

- ○ have to provide somewhat stronger evidence than now linking
- ○ have to provide somewhat stronger evidence than they do now and link
- ○ would have to provide somewhat stronger evidence than they do now and link
- ○ would have to provide somewhat stronger evidence than they do now linking
- ○ would have to provide somewhat stronger evidence than now linking

ASTEROID THEORY

To popularize the asteroid theory of dinosaur extinction, paleontologists <u>have to provide somewhat stronger evidence than now linking</u> the disappearance of fossil records and the layer of sediment in the Earth's crust caused by an asteroid impact.

o   have to provide somewhat stronger evidence than now linking
o   have to provide somewhat stronger evidence than they do now and link
o   would have to provide somewhat stronger evidence than they do now and link
o   would have to provide somewhat stronger evidence than they do now linking
o   would have to provide somewhat stronger evidence than now linking

EXPLANATION

Creating a filter: The sentence as written has a comparison. "Stronger evidence than now." The written form isn't expressing the intended meaning, because it's comparing evidence with a time (now, that is). It intends to compare stronger evidence with the evidence provided now. That bit of extra wording is required to convey the idea precisely, so we go off looking for it in the answer choices.

Applying the filter: (B) through (D) all solve that problem. (B) and (C) both end with "and link." That phrasing distorts the intended meaning, because it says not that the evidence is doing the linking, but rather that the paleontologists are linking. The correct answer is (D).

Although his approval rating is at an all-time low, the candidate's remarks aired in tonight's press conference seem <u>like it is suggestive that</u> his bid for reelection, previously thought improbable, is all but inevitable.

- ○ like it is suggestive that
- ○ as if to suggest
- ○ to suggest that
- ○ suggestive of
- ○ like a suggestion for

CANDIDATE'S REMARKS

Although his approval rating is at an all-time low, the candidate's remarks aired in tonight's press conference seem <u>like it is suggestive that</u> his bid for reelection, previously thought improbable, is all but inevitable.

- ○ like it is suggestive that
- ○ as if to suggest
- ○ to suggest that
- ○ suggestive of
- ○ like a suggestion for

EXPLANATION

Creating a filter: In this question, the phrase "like it is suggestive" is redundant, or maybe nonsensical. Is it actually suggestive, or is it merely *like* it is suggestive?

Applying the filter: Choice (B) has a similar problem because "as if" is used when something is contrary to fact and that's not the meaning here. For example, it would make sense to say the candidate was acting "as if he were going to run for reelection," if, in fact, he wasn't. Choice (D) is wrong because the preposition "of" cannot introduce a clause, only a noun. Choice (E) has the same problem as (D) and also changes the meaning of the sentence, since a "suggestion" is a recommendation. Choice (C) works nicely because it is succinct and introduces the clause (about what is being suggested) properly with the word "that." The correct answer is (C).

Bertrand Russell carried on the fledgling tradition <u>of the philosophy of logic, in both its goals and in methods, but he had been</u> ultimately no more successful than his predecessor Gottlob Frege in attempts to ground arithmetic in the precepts of formal logic.

- ○ of the philosophy of logic, in both its goals and in methods, but he had been
- ○ of the philosophy of logic, in both its goals and methods, but he was
- ○ of the philosophy of logic, not only in its goals and methods, but he was
- ○ of the philosophy of logic, in its goals and in also methods, but he was
- ○ of the philosophy of logic, not only in its goals and methods, but he had also been

BERTRAND RUSSELL

Bertrand Russell carried on the fledgling tradition <u>of the philosophy of logic, in both its goals and in methods, but he had been</u> ultimately no more successful than his predecessor Gottlob Frege in attempts to ground arithmetic in the precepts of formal logic.

○   of the philosophy of logic, in both its goals and in methods, but he had been
○   of the philosophy of logic, in both its goals and methods, but he was
○   of the philosophy of logic, not only in its goals and methods, but he was
○   of the philosophy of logic, in its goals and in also methods, but he was
○   of the philosophy of logic, not only in its goals and methods, but he had also been

EXPLANATION

Creating a filter: in this question, when we read the prompt, we pause at "had been." We're always suspicious of the past perfect, because it's overused. For it to be warranted, the action had to happen before something else. But before what, in this case? Not the "carrying on." He was no more successful, *ultimately* — that is, *after* he had carried on the tradition, not before. Gottlob Frege, similarly, came before the ultimate lack of success, not after. Drawing a timeline with the events on it can clarify this; the past perfect tense has to come to the left of an event in the simple past tense.

Applying the filter: So, fixing the tense, the answer is (B). Choice (E) has the same tense problem as the original sentence. Choices (C) and (D) both distort the intended meaning by messing around with the expression of goals and methods. The correct answer is (B).

Although Japanese encephalitis often results in only mild symptoms, <u>its symptoms are so severe and intractable that one in four cases</u> are fatal.

- ○ its symptoms are so severe and intractable that one in four cases
- ○ it is of such severity and intractability, one in four cases
- ○ so severe and intractable is it such that one in four cases
- ○ such is its severity and intractability, one of four cases
- ○ there is so much severity and intractability that one of four cases

JAPANESE ENCEPHALITIS

Although Japanese encephalitis often results in only mild symptoms, <u>its symptoms are so severe and intractable that one in four cases</u> are fatal.

○   its symptoms are so severe and intractable that one in four cases
○   it is of such severity and intractability, one in four cases
○   so severe and intractable is it such that one in four cases
○   such is its severity and intractability, one of four cases
○   there is so much severity and intractability that one of four cases

EXPLANATION

Creating a filter: no error jumps out in the sentence. "So that" is a valid idiom. We'll try to eliminate the other answer choices by finding objective defects.

Choice (B) introduces wordiness with no gain, and without a "that" in place of a comma, it creates a run-on sentence. In (C), "it is such that" is not a valid phrase and uses a pronoun that has no reference. Choice (D) has the same problems as (B). "Severity and intractability" would appear to describe the *kind* of severity, not the degree. (E) is not a run-on, but it describes severity and intractability as if they are easily quantifiable (with "so much") and generally present around us (with "there is"). The correct answer is (A).

Japan has a land area <u>similar to California but fully 128 million in population, where</u> 23% are over the age of 65, according to the 2010 census.

○ about the same as California but fully 128 million in population, where 23%
○ of a similar size as California is, but in Japan there is a population of fully 128 million, and
○ that is about the same size as California's land area, but in Japan with a population of fully 128 million people, of them
○ similar to the size of California, but fully 128 million in population, and
○ similar to that of California but a population of fully 128 million people, of whom

JAPAN'S LAND AREA

Japan has a land area <u>similar to California but fully 128 million in population, where</u> 23% are over the age of 65, according to the 2010 census.

○   about the same as California but fully 128 million in population, where 23%
○   of a similar size as California is, but in Japan there is a population of fully 128 million, and
○   that is about the same size as California's land area, but in Japan with a population of fully 128 million people, of them
○   similar to the size of California, but fully 128 million in population, and
○   similar to that of California but a population of fully 128 million people, of whom

EXPLANATION

Creating a filter: the original version of the sentence sounds poor, but so poor that it's probably easier just to go straight to the answer choices. The answer choices are diverse, so we can start with (B) and examine them one at a time.

Finding objective defects: choice (B) has a bad comparison between "similar size" and "California." We can't compare a size with a country, so (B) is out. In (C), the comparison is improved, but the phrase "but in Japan with" is redundant and awkward. Choice (D) sets apart the phrase starting with "but fully..." with a comma as if it's an independent clause, but it has no verb, so it is grammatically not viable. Choice (E) works: the comparison is correct, because "that" stands for "land area", and "of whom" refers to the population. Back to (A). Does (A) have an error? Yes; the word "where" does not actually refer to a place, as it must, but to a population. The correct answer is (E).

The Association of Southeast Asian Nations was not established to draw its member nations into a close economic and political union; it will strengthen its charter <u>someday, but only if leading members, including Singapore, Indonesia, and Thailand, were to place pressure</u> on the smaller members to yield to the common interest.

- ○ someday, but only if leading members, including Singapore, Indonesia, and Thailand, were to place pressure
- ○ someday, but only if pressure from leading members, including Singapore, Indonesia, and Thailand, is placed
- ○ someday only if leading members, including Singapore, Indonesia, and Thailand, would place pressure
- ○ someday only if leading members, which includes Singapore, Indonesia, and Thailand, were placing pressure
- ○ someday only if leading members, including Singapore, Indonesia, and Thailand, place pressure

THE ASSOCIATION OF SOUTHEAST ASIAN NATIONS

The Association of Southeast Asian Nations was not established to draw its member nations into a close economic and political union; it will strengthen its charter <u>someday, but only if leading members, including Singapore, Indonesia, and Thailand, were to place pressure</u> on the smaller members to yield to the common interest.

- ○ someday, but only if leading members, including Singapore, Indonesia, and Thailand, were to place pressure
- ○ someday, but only if pressure from leading members, including Singapore, Indonesia, and Thailand, is placed   *Passive*
- ○ someday only if leading members, including Singapore, Indonesia, and Thailand, <u>would</u> place pressure   (?)
- ○ someday only if leading members, which includes Singapore, Indonesia, and Thailand, <u>were</u> placing pressure
- ○ someday only if leading members, including Singapore, Indonesia, and Thailand, place pressure

EXPLANATION

   Creating a filter: In this question, when we read the prompt, we pause about the relationship between the word "if" and the word "were." As usual, we're checking not just for grammar, but to identify what the intended meaning of the sentence is and whether it's expressed. The word "if" identifies a condition. "Were" is a verb in the subjunctive mood, which in this case, is expressing a condition contrary to fact. Those two things could go together. We could say, "if we were king, we would do X, Y, and Z." But this is a statement about the future. The words "will strengthen" and "someday" make that clear. And in the future, the condition doesn't go along with the contrary to fact. It's a fact: if these countries place pressure, they will strengthen their charter.

   Applying the filter: This leads us to answer choice (E). Choice (B) uses the passive tense without need. Choice (C) uses "would" inside the condition, which doesn't make sense here. (D) has the same problem as (A). The answer is (E). Notice that the word "but" isn't needed. The phrase "only if" is accurate and complete in identifying the necessary condition for the strengthening of the charter. The correct answer is (E).

The seeming absence in the universe of a quantity of mass required to explain various phenomena, specifically gravitational effects, <u>believed to be</u> evidence for the existence of dark matter.

- ○ believed to be
- ○ is believed to be
- ○ some believe it to be
- ○ some believe it is
- ○ it is believed that it is

MISSING MATTER

The seeming absence in the universe of a quantity of mass required to explain various phenomena, specifically gravitational effects, <u>believed to be</u> evidence for the existence of dark matter.

- ○ believed to be
- ○ is believed to be
- ○ some believe it to be
- ○ some believe it is
- ○ it is believed that it is

EXPLANATION

Creating a filter: When we read the prompt, we can imagine it to be without the appositive phrase, "specifically gravitational effects," and the prepositional phrase before the comma all the way back to "in the universe," since such phrases can be removed without altering the grammar around it. That gives us, "the seeming absence... believed to be." We are missing a verb, an "is."

Applying the filter: our expectation is present in answer choice (B). Note that choices (C) through (E) all set up a proper subject-verb pair for the latter clause of the sentence, but they leave the original subject "absence" without a verb. The correct answer is (B).

verb

In 1646, William Stafford published *The Reason of the War, with the Progress and Accidents Thereof, Written by an English Subject*, <u>arguing in a pamphlet that Charles I give more power to Parliament</u> and for peace on the basis of constitutional monarchy.

○   arguing in a pamphlet that Charles I give more power to Parliament
○   arguing in a pamphlet for more power to Parliament from Charles I
○   a pamphlet advocating greater parliamentary powers from Charles I
○   a pamphlet advocating that Charles I give more power to Parliament
○   a pamphlet that argued for Charles I to give more power to Parliament

STAFFORD'S PAMPHLET

In 1646, William Stafford published *The Reason of the War, with the Progress and Accidents Thereof, Written by an English Subject*, <u>arguing in a pamphlet that Charles I give more power to Parliament</u> and for peace on the basis of constitutional monarchy.

- ○ arguing in a pamphlet that Charles I give more power to Parliament
- ○ arguing in a pamphlet for more power to Parliament from Charles I
- ○ a pamphlet advocating greater parliamentary powers from Charles I
- ○ a pamphlet advocating that Charles I give more power to Parliament
- ○ a pamphlet that argued for Charles I to give more power to Parliament

EXPLANATION

Creating a filter: if we don't draw any immediate conclusions from the prompt, we can go to the answer choices.

Finding objective defects: the answer choices naturally fall into two groups, one containing (A) and (B), and the second containing (C) through (E). We have to be careful about the modifying phrase that starts with "arguing" in the original sentence. It's unclear in its reference, because it comes after and therefore modifies the pamphlet, but says "arguing *in a pamphlet*" as if modifying Stafford. Better to have it clearly modify the pamphlet. That decision limits us to (C) through (E). Choice (C) uses the phrase "powers from"; this is non-idiomatic English without a verb prior to "powers." You could say you "advocate a *transfer* of power from X to Y," but to say you "advocate power from X" isn't sensible English. Choice (C) is further twisted because the powers are identified as "parliamentary" in a way that doesn't make it clear that they are initially *not* parliamentary. So (C) is out. Choice (D) has a good feature, which is to introduce the thing being advocated in a clause after the word "that"; we generally favor that construction. But here, that construction is not parallel with the phrase "and for peace..." later in the sentence. Choice (E) is parallel in that way: the pamphlet argues *for* one thing and *for* another. The correct answer is (E).

The events of the 2006 movie *Driving Lessons* focus on the <u>friendship between Ben, a shy teenaged boy, with an aging and eccentric actress, Evie,</u> when she hires the boy as a companion to assist her in the house and drive her to various appointments.

- friendship between Ben, a shy teenaged boy, with an aging and eccentric actress, Evie,
- friends Ben, a shy teenaged boy, along with an aging and eccentric actress, Evie,
- friendship that develops between Ben, a shy teenaged boy, and an aging and eccentric actress, Evie,
- developing friendship between Ben, a shy teenaged boy, with an aging and eccentric actress, Evie,
- shy teenaged boy, Ben, and the friendship with an aging and eccentric actress, Evie,

DRIVING LESSONS

The events of the 2006 movie *Driving Lessons* focus on the <u>friendship between Ben, a shy teenaged boy, with an aging and eccentric actress, Evie,</u> when she hires the boy as a companion to assist her in the house and drive her to various appointments.

o   friendship between Ben, a shy teenaged boy, with an aging and eccentric actress, Evie,

o   friends Ben, a shy teenaged boy, along with an aging and eccentric actress, Evie,

o   friendship that develops between Ben, a shy teenaged boy, and an aging and eccentric actress, Evie,

o   developing friendship between Ben, a shy teenaged boy, with an aging and eccentric actress, Evie,

o   shy teenaged boy, Ben, and the friendship with an aging and eccentric actress, Evie,

EXPLANATION

Creating a filter: We read the prompt and spot a problem. "Between" requires the use of "and," not "with." **"Between...and..." is a key two-part construction on the GMAT.** We look for an answer choice that solves the problem.

Applying the filter: our filter applies most quickly to Choice (C), which solves the problem, and choice (D), which does not. We'll check (B) and (E). In (B), "along with" is wordy and grammatically removes "Evie" from part of "friends," so it's out. In (E), Ben has now been removed from the friendship. The correct answer is (C).

style

Idiom

Download the free SC Strategy Sheets at GMATFree.com/SC-Strategy-Sheets

In 1021, Murasaki Shikibu completed <u>The Tale of Genji, a work that, spanning over 50 chapters and 400 characters, and which many scholars, judging its psychological complexity, consider</u> the first novel.

- ○ *The Tale of Genji,* a work that, spanning over 50 chapters and 400 characters, and which many scholars, judging its psychological complexity, consider
- ○ *The Tale of Genji*, a work that spans over 50 chapters and 400 characters and which many scholars, judging its psychological complexity, consider
- ○ *The Tale of Genji*, a work that had spanned over 50 chapters and 400 characters and which many scholars, judging its psychological complexity, consider it as
- ○ her crafting of *The Tale of Genji*, a work spanning over 50 chapters and 400 characters and which many scholars, judging its psychological complexity, consider it as
- ○ her crafting of *The Tale of Genji*, a work spanning over 50 chapters and 400 characters and which many scholars, judging its psychological complexity, consider it

In 1021, Murasaki Shikibu completed _The Tale of Genji,_ <u>a work that, spanning over 50 chapters and 400 characters, and which many scholars, judging its psychological complexity, consider</u> the first novel.

- ○ _The Tale of Genji,_ a work that, spanning over 50 chapters and 400 characters, and which many scholars, judging its psychological complexity, consider
- ○ _The Tale of Genji_, a work that spans over 50 chapters and 400 characters and which many scholars, judging its psychological complexity, consider
- ○ _The Tale of Genji_, a work that had spanned over 50 chapters and 400 characters and which many scholars, judging its psychological complexity, consider it as
- ○ her crafting of _The Tale of Genji_, a work spanning over 50 chapters and 400 characters and which many scholars, judging its psychological complexity, consider it as
- ○ her crafting of _The Tale of Genji_, a work spanning over 50 chapters and 400 characters and which many scholars, judging its psychological complexity, consider it

EXPLANATION

Creating a filter: there's a problem with the original sentence. The phrase "a work that" is never completed with a verb. The "spanning" and "judging" phrases can be omitted and "consider" goes with "scholars." We will go to the answer choices with the aim to fix this problem.

Applying the filter: There is a 3 versus 2 grouping of answer choices, evident in the first words of each line. Choices (A) through (C) are clearer. In choices (D) and (E), the phrase "her crafting of" is needlessly wordy, and, even worse, an ungrammatical redundancy is set up between the relative pronoun "which" and the pronoun "it," both of which refer to the book. That leaves us with (B) and (C). Between (B) and (C), the present tense makes more sense, as the work still spans 50 chapters; the 50 chapters are a permanent property of the book, a timeless fact, and **general, timeless facts are best expressed in the present tense.** The correct answer is (B).

According to the nineteenth-century schema of a "well-made play," <u>all of the happenings on stage are driven by a single discovery, such as that of a letter, and when they follow from it in a series of events, often involving misinterpretations by the characters.</u>

○   all of the happenings on stage are driven by a single discovery, such as that of a letter, and when they follow from it in a series of events, often involving misinterpretations by the characters

○   all of the happenings on stage are driven by a single discovery, such as that of a letter, and by the series of events, often involving misinterpretations by the characters, that follows from it

○   all of the happenings on stage are driven by a single discovery, such as that of a letter, as well as the series of events, often involving misinterpretations by the characters, that follows from it

○   a single discovery, such as that of a letter, drives all of the happenings on stage, and also the series of events, often involving misinterpretations by the characters, that follow from it

○   the discovery of a single item such a letter drives all of the happenings on stage, as well as the series of events, often involving misinterpretations by the characters, that follow from it

WELL-MADE PLAY

According to the nineteenth-century schema of a "well-made play," <u>all of the happenings on stage are driven by a single discovery, such as that of a letter, and when they follow from it in a series of events, often involving misinterpretations by the characters.</u>

o   all of the happenings on stage are driven by a single discovery, such as that of a letter, and when they follow from it in a series of events, often involving misinterpretations by the characters

o   all of the happenings on stage are driven by a single discovery, such as that of a letter, and by the series of events, often involving misinterpretations by the characters, that follows from it

o   all of the happenings on stage are driven by a single discovery, such as that of a letter, as well as the series of events, often involving misinterpretations by the characters, that follows from it

o   a single discovery, such as that of a letter, drives all of the happenings on stage, and also the series of events, often involving misinterpretations by the characters, that follow from it

o   the discovery of a single item such a letter drives all of the happenings on stage, as well as the series of events, often involving misinterpretations by the characters, that follow from it

EXPLANATION

Creating a filter: The prompt gets awkward and imprecise around the phrase, "when they follow from it in a series of events." We will hold (A) in contempt and examine the others, especially for options that handle the pronouns more clearly and get rid of the "when," because we are not talking about a time.

Applying the filter: preferring the active voice, we might start with (D) and (E). But in (E), "single item" is redundant, and "as well as" is a phrase that should almost never be used. In (D), it seems redundant to drive all of the happenings *and* the series of events that follow from the discovery. Choice (C) also has the dreaded "as well as," which also introduces ambiguity about what role the "series of events" is playing. (B) is clearer: all the events are driven by one of two things, the discovery, and the series of events that follows from it. Choice (B) uses passive voice, but it's the only one to convey the meaning correctly. A defense of the use of passive voice here is that it allows the author of the sentence to put the ideas of the sentence in an order that is easier to understand. The correct answer is (B).

The ministry asserts that improvements in sentiment indicators are evidence <u>that the economy will dodge the uncertainty that had been caused earlier by the euro debt crisis and instead grow</u> by 1.8 percent in 2014.

- o that the economy will dodge the uncertainty that had been caused earlier by the euro debt crisis and instead grow
- o in the economy to dodge the uncertainty, what the euro debt crisis caused earlier, rather to grow
- o in the economy's ability to dodge the uncertainty, something earlier the euro debt crisis caused, and instead to grow
- o in the economy to dodge the uncertainty the euro debt crisis caused earlier, and rather to grow
- o that the economy will dodge the uncertainty the euro debt crisis had caused earlier, with it instead growing

THE MINISTRY ASSERTS

The ministry asserts that improvements in sentiment indicators are evidence <u>that the economy will dodge the uncertainty that had been caused earlier by the euro debt crisis and instead grow</u> by 1.8 percent in 2014.

○ that the economy will dodge the uncertainty that had been caused earlier by the euro debt crisis and instead grow
○ in the economy to dodge the uncertainty, what the euro debt crisis caused earlier, rather to grow
○ in the economy's ability to dodge the uncertainty, something earlier the euro debt crisis caused, and instead to grow
○ in the economy to dodge the uncertainty the euro debt crisis caused earlier, and rather to grow
○ that the economy will dodge the uncertainty the euro debt crisis had caused earlier, with it instead growing

EXPLANATION

Creating a filter: when we read the prompt, maybe it has no error, so we go on to the answer choices.

Applying the filter: we have a 2 versus 3 grouping in how the answer choices begin. We are talking about evidence that supports a claim; the best way to introduce the claim is with the word "that." That leaves us with (A) and (E). Choice (E) has an objectionable phrase "with it instead growing." "With" is not properly a conjunction, and it's being used as one here. We review (B) through (D) to establish further that the wording is awkward, beyond the problem with them already mentioned. The correct answer is (A).

It is not in fact a whale, but the whale shark is as large as some species of whales, which measures up to 42 feet from tooth to fin.

○ It is not in fact a whale, but the whale shark is as large as some species of whales, which measures

○ Although it is not in fact a whale, the whale shark is as large as some species of whales, which measures

○ Not in fact a whale, the whale shark is as large as some species of whales, measuring

○ Though not in fact a whale but it is as large as some species of whales, the whale shark measures

○ Despite not being in fact a whale, the whale shark is as large as some species of whales, measuring

WHALE SHARK

<u>It is not in fact a whale, but the whale shark is as large as some species of whales, which measures</u> up to 42 feet from tooth to fin.

- ○ It is not in fact a whale, but the whale shark is as large as some species of whales, which measures
- ○ Although it is not in fact a whale, the whale shark is as large as some species of whales, which measures
- ○ Not in fact a whale, the whale shark is as large as some species of whales, measuring
- ○ Though not in fact a whale but it is as large as some species of whales, the whale shark measures
- ○ Despite not being in fact a whale, the whale shark is as large as some species of whales, measuring

EXPLANATION

Creating a filter: there's a problem with the original sentence: the phrase "which measures" appears to point back to "species of whales," but that's against the intended meaning of the sentence.

Applying the filter: scanning the answer choices, we see (B) retains the problem, so (B) is out. Choice (D) has defects: "though not in fact a whale" should modify a noun set off by a comma but instead drives into a clause with a subordinate conjunction; that's ungrammatical. Choice (E) is an inferior version of (C) with an unnecessary gerund, "being." The correct answer is (C).

The first shinkansen, or bullet train, which was built in time for the first Tokyo Olympics, reduced <u>from 6 hours and 40 minutes to just four hours the required time of traveling from Tokyo to Osaka</u>.

○ from 6 hours and 40 minutes to just four hours the required time of traveling from Tokyo to Osaka
○ the time being required to travel from Tokyo to Osaka, from 6 hours and 40 minutes down to just four hours
○ the time being required to travel from Tokyo to Osaka, 6 hours and 40 minutes to just four hours
○ the time required to travel from Tokyo to Osaka from 6 hours and 40 minutes to just four hours
○ from 6 hours and 40 minutes to just four hours, the time required to travel from Tokyo to Osaka

SHINKANSEN

The first shinkansen, or bullet train, which was built in time for the first Tokyo Olympics, reduced <u>from 6 hours and 40 minutes to just four hours the required time of traveling from Tokyo to Osaka</u>.

- ○ from 6 hours and 40 minutes to just four hours the required time of traveling from Tokyo to Osaka
- ○ the time being required to travel from Tokyo to Osaka, from 6 hours and 40 minutes down to just four hours
- ○ the time being required to travel from Tokyo to Osaka, 6 hours and 40 minutes to just four hours
- ○ the time required to travel from Tokyo to Osaka from 6 hours and 40 minutes to just four hours
- ○ from 6 hours and 40 minutes to just four hours, the time required to travel from Tokyo to Osaka

EXPLANATION

Creating a filter: the sentence as written has the phrase "the required time of traveling," which sounds unnatural. We examine how that phrase is handled in the other answer choices.

Applying the filter: choices (B) and (C) make the situation even worse by including the gerund "being" unnecessarily. Choice (E) has a strange word order, and it also creates a grammatical error by separating subject and verb by a single comma. The correct answer is (D).

<u>To Dr. Charles Lauritsen and Commander Sherman Burroughs, the Mojave could house a naval facility long before the desert was commonly thought of for such uses,</u> and in 1943 the Navy established the area of China Lake as a naval ordnance test station.

- To Dr. Charles Lauritsen and Commander Sherman Burroughs, the Mojave could house a naval facility long before the desert was commonly thought of for such uses,
- To Dr. Charles Lauritsen and Commander Sherman Burroughs, long before the desert was commonly thought of for such uses, the Mojave could house a naval facility,
- Dr. Charles Lauritsen and Commander Sherman Burroughs chose the Mojave to house a naval facility before the desert was commonly thought of for such uses,
- Long before the desert was commonly thought of for such uses, Dr. Charles Lauritsen and Commander Sherman Burroughs chose the Mojave to house a naval facility,
- Long before the desert was commonly thought of being for such uses, the Mojave was chosen by Dr. Charles Lauritsen and Commander Sherman Burroughs to house a naval facility,

MOJAVE FACILITY

<u>To Dr. Charles Lauritsen and Commander Sherman Burroughs, the Mojave could house a naval facility long before the desert was commonly thought of for such uses,</u> and in 1943 the Navy established the area of China Lake as a naval ordnance test station.

○   To Dr. Charles Lauritsen and Commander Sherman Burroughs, the Mojave could house a naval facility long before the desert was commonly thought of for such uses,

○   To Dr. Charles Lauritsen and Commander Sherman Burroughs, long before the desert was commonly thought of for such uses, the Mojave could house a naval facility,

○   Dr. Charles Lauritsen and Commander Sherman Burroughs chose the Mojave to house a naval facility before the desert was commonly thought of for such uses,

○   Long before the desert was commonly thought of for such uses, Dr. Charles Lauritsen and Commander Sherman Burroughs chose the Mojave to house a naval facility,

○   Long before the desert was commonly thought of being for such uses, the Mojave was chosen by Dr. Charles Lauritsen and Commander Sherman Burroughs to house a naval facility,

EXPLANATION

Creating a filter: At first glance, the prompt may seem strange, though it may be difficult to say why. Let's review the answer choices and look for objective defects.

Applying the filter: (B) is worse than (A) and has an objective problem because it's unclear whether the phrase starting with "long before" modifies what comes before it or after it. So (B) is out. (C) seems pretty clear and is a more direct wording. (E) is definitely worse than (D) because it uses the passive tense unnecessarily. So we're comparing (C) and (D) and we are holding (A) under suspicion. The problem with (A), come to think of it, is the use of "to," which is awkward, and (A) also miscommunicates the "long before" part — it sounds ambiguously like part of their belief rather than the timing of their belief. That can help us realize that (C) also has that problem: "Before the desert was commonly thought of for such uses" – does that modify the choosing or the housing? Choice (C) is therefore out. The correct answer is (D).

A study concludes that the Indus civilization, which existed 6,000 years ago, experienced violence and disease of such severity <u>they eroded the ability of the population to stay in their cities and, the result is, to remain</u> intact as a civilization.

- ○ they eroded the ability of the population to stay in their cities and, the result is, to remain
- ○ that they eroded the ability of the population to stay in their cities and, as a result, to remain
- ○ that they eroded the ability of the population to stay in their cities and, the result of this, they were unable to remain
- ○ that they eroded the ability of the population to stay in their cities, and resulted in being unable to remain
- ○ as to erode the ability of the population for staying in their cities, resulting in being unable to remain

INDUS CIVILIZATION

A study concludes that the Indus civilization, which existed 6,000 years ago, experienced violence and disease of such severity <u>they eroded the ability of the population to stay in their cities and, the result is, to remain</u> intact as a civilization.

- o they eroded the ability of the population to stay in their cities and, the result is, to remain
- o that they eroded the ability of the population to stay in their cities and, as a result, to remain
- o that they eroded the ability of the population to stay in their cities and, the result of this, they were unable to remain
- o that they eroded the ability of the population to stay in their cities, and resulted in being unable to remain
- o as to erode the ability of the population for staying in their cities, resulting in being unable to remain

EXPLANATION

Creating a filter: in the sentence as written, the first thing we notice is that the word "that" is missing: "such severity *that* they." Our ear tells us this and "such... that" is a prior idiom.

Applying the filter: choices (B) through (D) fix the problem in the way we expect. (C) has an unnecessary pronoun with no reference in "this," and (D) has an unnecessary gerund "being." Both (C) and (D) also have basic errors in connecting clauses with conjunctions: (C) throws one into the middle of the sentence as if it were an appositive, which it isn't, and (D) inserts a comma without adding or re-mentioning the subject. Choice (E) is missing the word "that" and includes the gerund "being" without cause. The correct answer is (B).

Galileo Galilei published his theory of the movement of planets in "Dialogue Concerning the Two Chief World Systems," <u>an attack on the Ptolemaic conception of the Sun's motion as well as an exposition of his</u> new theory to replace it.

- ○ an attack on the Ptolemaic conception of the Sun's motion as well as an exposition of his
- ○ an attack on the Ptolemaic conception of the Sun's motion and his expositing of a
- ○ an attack on the Ptolemaic conception of the Sun's motion and expositing as well
- ○ attacking the Ptolemaic conception of the Sun's motion and also an exposition of his
- ○ attacking the Ptolemaic conception of the Sun's motion as well as the expositing of his

GALILEO'S ATTACK

Galileo Galilei published his theory of the movement of planets in "Dialogue Concerning the Two Chief World Systems," <u>an attack on the Ptolemaic conception of the Sun's motion as well as an exposition of his</u> new theory to replace it.

○   an attack on the Ptolemaic conception of the Sun's motion as well as an exposition of his
○   an attack on the Ptolemaic conception of the Sun's motion and his expositing of a
○   an attack on the Ptolemaic conception of the Sun's motion and expositing as well
○   attacking the Ptolemaic conception of the Sun's motion and also an exposition of his
○   attacking the Ptolemaic conception of the Sun's motion as well as the expositing of his

EXPLANATION

Creating a filter: The prompt starts out well but runs into problems with "as well as," a phrase that is rarely well used. We check out the answer choices looking for better options.

Applying the filter: we find bigger defects; there are parallelism problems with the attacking and the expositing all over the place here. Choices (B) through (E) all fail to be parallel. Choice (E) looks close but the article "the" before "expositing" makes it a noun and ruins it. The correct answer is (A). We could defend the "as well as" the way it's written as needed to remove ambiguity and clarify that the Dialogue wasn't an attack on the exposition, but it doesn't matter, as long as we find objective grounds for our answer. The correct answer is (A).

Golf clubs with graphite shafts are favored by many less experienced players to maximize their shot's <u>distance, designed to be both lightweight and to take</u> less force to swing.

- ○ distance, designed to be both lightweight and to take
- ○ distance, designed to be both lightweight and take
- ○ distance, both designed to be lightweight and to take
- ○ distance and are both designed to be lightweight and to take
- ○ distance and are designed both to be lightweight and to take

GRAPHITE SHAFTS

Golf clubs with graphite shafts are favored by many less experienced players to maximize their shot's <u>distance, designed to be both lightweight and to take</u> less force to swing.

○ distance, designed to be both lightweight and to take
○ distance, designed to be both lightweight and take
○ distance, both designed to be lightweight and to take
○ distance and are both designed to be lightweight and to take
○ distance and are designed both to be lightweight and to take

EXPLANATION

Creating a filter: in this question, we might get tripped up in reading the original sentence right around the comma after "distance." The phrase starting with "designed" sounds as if it is modifying "distance," counter to the intended meaning. We can probably find an answer choice that expresses the intended meaning more clearly.

Applying the filter: Choices (D) and (E) dispel the problem. Choice (D) puts "both" in the wrong place and (E) has it in the right place. It's only designed once but for two purposes, so "both" should be right after "designed." In fact, (E) is the only answer choice that has that detail correct. The correct answer is (E).

The analysis recommended that management <u>should upgrade security cameras, improve fire equipment, and increase the presence of security guards</u>.

- O should upgrade security cameras, improve fire equipment, and increase the presence of security guards
- O should upgrade security cameras, fire equipment should be improved, and the presence of security guards should be increased
- O to upgrade security cameras, to improve fire equipment, and to increase the presence of security guards
- O upgrade security cameras, improve fire equipment, and the presence of security guards increased
- O upgrade security cameras, improve fire equipment, and increase the presence of security guards

MANAGEMENT RECOMMENDATIONS

The analysis recommended that management <u>should upgrade security cameras, improve fire equipment, and increase the presence of security guards</u>.

- ○ should upgrade security cameras, improve fire equipment, and increase the presence of security guards
- ○ should upgrade security cameras, fire equipment should be improved, and the presence of security guards should be increased
- ○ to upgrade security cameras, to improve fire equipment, and to increase the presence of security guards
- ○ upgrade security cameras, improve fire equipment, and the presence of security guards increased
- ○ upgrade security cameras, improve fire equipment, and increase the presence of security guards

EXPLANATION

Creating a filter: In this question, when we read the prompt, quite possibly no error jumps out. It's a parallel list of verbs. So we can turn to the answer choices, systematically.

Finding objective defects: choice (B) has unnecessary passive voice, so it's out. In (C), the infinitives don't follow "recommended that" according to English idiom. (D) is not parallel. (E) sounds good, better than we expected. Comparing (E) and (A), we can see the word "should" shouldn't be present here. This is one of the rare cases in English other than contrary-to-fact situations in which the subjunctive mood is used. Subjunctive mood is used in some cases in which an order or recommendation is given. It hinges primarily on the verb. Some proper usages (with subjunctive used in the last one only) are: *It told management to upgrade; it said that management should upgrade; it recommended that management upgrade.* The correct answer is (E).

Tax evasion and fraud are wealth distortion <u>mechanisms that enable the owners and controllers of wealth to escape their responsibilities to society and to be able to continue to accumulate</u> wealth with the support that same society.

○ mechanisms that enable the owners and controllers of wealth to escape their responsibilities to society and to be able to continue to accumulate

○ mechanisms that enable the owners and controllers of wealth to escape their responsibilities to society and to continue to accumulate

○ mechanisms; that enable the owners and controllers of wealth to escape their responsibilities to society, to continue to accumulate

○ mechanisms, which enables the owners and controllers of wealth to escape their responsibilities to society, accumulating

○ programs, which enable the owners and controllers of wealth to be able to escape their responsibilities to society, continuing to accumulate

WEALTH DISTORTION MECHANISMS

Tax evasion and fraud are wealth distortion <u>mechanisms that enable the owners and controllers of wealth to escape their responsibilities to society and to be able to continue to accumulate</u> wealth with the support that same society.

- ○ mechanisms that enable the owners and controllers of wealth to escape their responsibilities to society and to be able to continue to accumulate
- ○ mechanisms that enable the owners and controllers of wealth to escape their responsibilities to society and to continue to accumulate
- ○ mechanisms; that enable the owners and controllers of wealth to escape their responsibilities to society, to continue to accumulate
- ○ mechanisms, which enables the owners and controllers of wealth to escape their responsibilities to society, accumulating
- ○ programs, which enable the owners and controllers of wealth to be able to escape their responsibilities to society, continuing to accumulate

EXPLANATION

Creating a filter: in this question, the phrase "to be able to continue" is defective, because "to be able" is redundant with "enable," which comes earlier in the sentence and governs the infinitive "to be able." At that point in the sentence we are still within the scope of what's "enabled."

Applying the filter, we'll consider (A) out and scan for other answer choices we can eliminate on the same grounds; the only one is (E).

Further notes: (B) is essentially a corrected version of (A). (C) has an improper semicolon usage; semicolons are used to connect two independent clauses without a conjunction. Choice (D) also is flawed, most obviously because "enables" is grammatically singular and can't match anything that comes with it. The correct answer is (B).

to be able → Redundant

Sir William Mills, the inventor of both the Mills bomb, the most widely hand grenade most widely used by British Imperial forces during the First World War, and <u>also of the Metallic Golfing Instrument Head, possibly the first aluminum golf club, was known as an innovative world-renowned inventor</u>.

- ○ also of the Metallic Golfing Instrument Head, possibly the first aluminum golf club, was known as an innovative world-renowned inventor
- ○ also the Metallic Golfing Instrument Head, possibly the first aluminum golf club, was known as an innovative world-renowned inventor
- ○ of the Metallic Golfing Instrument Head, which possibly was the first aluminum golf club, was a world-renowned inventor
- ○ of the Metallic Golfing Instrument Head, possibly the first aluminum golf club, was known as a world-renowned inventor
- ○ the Metallic Golfing Instrument Head, possibly the first aluminum golf club, was a world-renowned inventor

Sir William Mills, the inventor of both the Mills bomb, the most widely hand grenade most widely used by British Imperial forces during the First World War, and <u>also of the Metallic Golfing Instrument Head, possibly the first aluminum golf club, was known as an innovative world-renowned inventor</u>.

○   also of the Metallic Golfing Instrument Head, possibly the first aluminum golf club, was known as an innovative world-renowned inventor

○   also the Metallic Golfing Instrument Head, possibly the first aluminum golf club, was known as an innovative world-renowned inventor

○   of the Metallic Golfing Instrument Head, which possibly was the first aluminum golf club, was a world-renowned inventor

○   of the Metallic Golfing Instrument Head, possibly the first aluminum golf club, was known as a world-renowned inventor

○   the Metallic Golfing Instrument Head, possibly the first aluminum golf club, was a world-renowned inventor

EXPLANATION

Creating a filter: as we're reading through the prompt, there seem to be an awful lot of modifying phrases set off by commas, but we may not see a definitive error.

Finding objective defects: as we compare answer choices, we can notice that a key choice is whether we start with the word "of," "also," or "also of." The answer to that question is determined by the prior phrase, near the beginning of the sentence, "inventor of *both* the Mills bomb..." To finish that off that "both," we need an "and," which we get before the underlined portion. "Also" is redundant. And the word "of" is not permitted, because the first "of" comes *before* "both." That leaves only one possibility: the correct answer is (E).

Although virtually any animal or plant records older than about 10,000 years old are typically termed fossils, the type of tissue and that of the external substance obviously determines whether a particular specimen is trace, derived, subfossil, or something else.

- virtually any animal or plant records older than about 10,000 years old are typically termed fossils, the type of tissue and that of the external substance obviously determines
- virtually any animal or plant record older than about 10,000 years old is typically termed a fossil, their type of tissue and that of the external substance obviously determine
- virtually all animal or plant records older than about 10,000 years old are typically termed fossils, their types of tissue and of the external substance obviously determines
- virtually any animal or plant record older than about 10,000 years old is typically termed a fossil, the type of tissue and that of the external substance of a given specimen obviously determines
- virtually all animal or plant records older than about 10,000 years old are typically termed fossils, the type of tissue and that of the external substance obviously determine

FOSSIL CLASSIFICATION

Although <u>virtually any animal or plant records older than about 10,000 years old are typically termed fossils, the type of tissue and that of the external substance obviously determines</u> whether a particular specimen is trace, derived, subfossil, or something else.

- ○ virtually any animal or plant records older than about 10,000 years old are typically termed fossils, the type of tissue and that of the external substance obviously determines
- ○ virtually any animal or plant record older than about 10,000 years old is typically termed a fossil, their type of tissue and that of the external substance obviously determine
- ○ virtually all animal or plant records older than about 10,000 years old are typically termed fossils, their types of tissue and of the external substance obviously determines
- ○ virtually any animal or plant record older than about 10,000 years old is typically termed a fossil, the type of tissue and that of the external substance of a given specimen obviously determines
- ○ virtually all animal or plant records older than about 10,000 years old are typically termed fossils, the type of tissue and that of the external substance obviously determine

EXPLANATION

Creating a filter: as we do the basic subject-verb check in the independent clause, "records" matches with "are," but we might ask whether "records" should be singular, since a decision about whether a certain item is a fossil is probably made item by item. That's not a conclusive consideration, however, so we can look for other differences in the answer choices

Logical proof: choice (B) gives us the grammatically singular "record" and "fossil," but it messes things up by using the plural pronoun "their" without a plural referent, so it's out. Choice (C) uses "their" as well in "their types," and it's meant to refer afterward to the grammatically singular "specimen." So (C) is out. Choices (D) and (E) are both free of "their." Choice (D) gives us the singular "record" we're looking for and is otherwise similar to (A). But then (E) reveals that both (A) and (D) are flawed, because it has the proper verb "determine." That verb should be grammatically plural, to correspond to "type of tissue and that of the external substance." We missed that basic defunct in our first scan of the question but found it soon enough. The correct answer is (E).

That enthusiasts predicted that first-year sales of electric cars would be strong is no surprise that they were incorrect: the cars cost more than gasoline-fueled cars of similar performance.

o   That enthusiasts predicted that first-year sales of electric cars would be strong is no surprise that they were incorrect
o   That enthusiasts predicted that first-year sales of electric cars would be strong is no surprise to be incorrect
o   It is no surprise that enthusiasts were incorrect who predicted that first-year sales of electric cars would be strong
o   It is no surprise that enthusiasts were incorrect in predicting that first-year sales of electric cars would be strong
o   The fact that enthusiasts were incorrect in predicting that first-year sales of electric cars would be strong is no surprise

FIRST-YEAR SALES

<u>That enthusiasts predicted that first-year sales of electric cars would be strong is no surprise that they were incorrect</u>: the cars cost more than gasoline-fueled cars of similar performance.

- ○ That enthusiasts predicted that first-year sales of electric cars would be strong is no surprise that they were incorrect
- ○ That enthusiasts predicted that first-year sales of electric cars would be strong is no surprise to be incorrect
- ○ It is no surprise that enthusiasts were incorrect who predicted that first-year sales of electric cars would be strong
- ○ It is no surprise that enthusiasts were incorrect in predicting that first-year sales of electric cars would be strong
- ○ The fact that enthusiasts were incorrect in predicting that first-year sales of electric cars would be strong is no surprise

EXPLANATION

Creating a filter: the original sentence is problematic. It's not automatically wrong to have the subject of a sentence begin with the word "that." For example, something like the following would be fine: "That they predicted sales would be strong is no surprise." We can look for a simpler construction in the answer choices, maybe one like our example.

Applying the filter: none of the answer choices quite match our expectation. Choice (B), like (A), tries to fuse two sentences together ungrammatically. Choice (C) separates the modifying clause "who predicted..." from the noun it's supposed to modify, enthusiasts. Furthermore, (C) clouds the meaning of the sentence by leaving unclear what the enthusiasts were wrong about, since the "who" clause identifies who the scientists are, not how they were incorrect. So choices (A) through (C) are out. Choice (D) is inferior to our prediction, because it uses the somewhat colloquial pronoun "it." But choice (E) is worse in expressing the redundancy that a "fact...is no surprise." So we must eliminate choice (E), and we are left with (D). The correct answer is (D).

With broad, flat bodies and small heads, <u>the cockroach's durability is to the insect world what</u> the honey badger is to that of the mustelids.

- ○ the cockroach's durability is to the insect world what
- ○ the cockroach's durability is to the insect world like
- ○ the cockroach's durability is to the insect world just as
- ○ the durable cockroach is to the insect world similar to what
- ○ the durable cockroach is to the insect world what

Cockroach Durability

With broad, flat bodies and small heads, <u>the cockroach's durability is to the insect world what</u> the honey badger is to that of the mustelids.

○ the cockroach's durability is to the insect world what
○ the cockroach's durability is to the insect world like
○ the cockroach's durability is to the insect world just as
○ the durable cockroach is to the insect world similar to what
○ the durable cockroach is to the insect world what

Explanation

Creating a filter: The beginning of the sentence attacks us with a modification error. The noun that comes after the comma after "heads" is "durability," so the grammar of the sentence conveys that *durability* is what has broad, flat, heads.

Applying the filter, we look for the answer choices that dispel the problem, and those are (D) and (E). Choice (D) has a redundant construction with the word "similar," because the phrase "is to" has already set up a comparison. The correct answer is (E).

The festival of Songkran always brings widespread levity and a rush of visitors to <u>Thailand in that the throwing of water on others in the street is encouraged</u>.

- ○ Thailand in that the throwing of water on others in the street is encouraged
- ○ Thailand, encouraging throwing water on others in the street
- ○ Thailand, when they encourage throwing water on others in the street
- ○ Thailand, since the throwing of water on others in the street is encouraged
- ○ Thailand by encouragement to throw water on others in the street

SONGKRAN FESTIVAL

The festival of Songkran always brings widespread levity and a rush of visitors to <u>Thailand in that the throwing of water on others in the street is encouraged</u>.

- ○ Thailand in that the throwing of water on others in the street is encouraged
- ○ Thailand, encouraging throwing water on others in the street
- ○ Thailand, when they encourage throwing water on others in the street
- ○ Thailand, since the throwing of water on others in the street is encouraged
- ○ Thailand by encouragement to throw water on others in the street

EXPLANATION

Creating a filter: We read the sentence and we're not sure whether there is an error. So, we'll start with answer choice (B) and look for objective defects.

Finding objective defects: the grammar of choice (B) indicates that the festival is doing the encouraging, contrary to the intended meaning, so B is out. In (C), the word "when" is off, because Songkran properly is a festival, not a time. (D) is similar to (A). (E) is out because "by encouragement" is not a proper English expression.

So we're down to (A) and (D). Choice (D) has simple logic with cause and effect established by "since." It uses passive voice, but so does (A), and this is a case where passive voice makes some sense, because we don't really know who is doing the encouraging; it's a general phenomenon. Choice (A) uses the words "in that," which, on closer look, doesn't describe precisely the relationship between the levity and the water-throwing. The phrase "in that" is used to provide more detail or rephrasing something, but that's not the meaning here. The intended meaning is to give reasons and causes, so "since" is better. The correct answer is (D).

One of the most significant aspects of the act is that it empowers the province to try <u>and set restrictions for the amount that will be paid by the government</u> for a particular drug under this legislation.

- ○ and set restrictions for the amount that will be paid by the government
- ○ and set restrictions on the amount able to be paid by the government
- ○ setting restrictions for the amount the government is allowed to pay
- ○ to set restrictions on the amount capable of being paid by the government
- ○ to set restrictions on the amount that will be paid by the government

RESTRICTIONS OF THE ACT

One of the most significant aspects of the act is that it empowers the province to try <u>and set restrictions for the amount that will be paid by the government</u> for a particular drug under this legislation.

- o   and set restrictions for the amount that will be paid by the government
- o   and set restrictions on the amount able to be paid by the government
- o   setting restrictions for the amount the government is allowed to pay
- o   to set restrictions on the amount capable of being paid by the government
- o   to set restrictions on the amount that will be paid by the government

EXPLANATION

Creating a filter: the sentence as written has an error at "try and set," which is not an allowed phrase in precise English. It's one action, not two, and the action is "try to set."

Applying the filter: our filter points us to (D) and (E). Choice (D) uses the gerund "being paid" without need. Choice (E) has passive voice but looks good. We check (C) - is there definitely an objective defect in (C)? Yes: "restrictions for" is not the English idiom; it's "restrictions on." The correct answer is (E).

Note: there is a difference between "try setting" and "try to set." In the first case, we know that we'll be able to do the setting, we're "trying" it to see what the result will be. In the second case, we don't know whether we will be able to set in the first place, but we are attempting to do so.

Announcing further steps to combat the lowering global price of rubber, the Thai Deputy Farm Minister's measures were announced today for curbing global supply by cutting nearly 150,000 tons in trees over the next 14 months.

o Minister's measures were announced today for curbing global supply by cutting nearly 150,000 tons in trees over the next 14 months
o Minister's measures, which are to curb global supply by cutting nearly 150,000 tons in trees over the next 14 months, were announced today
o Minister's measures for curbing global supply by cutting nearly 150,000 tons in trees over the next 14 months were announced today
o Minister announced measures today to curb global supply by cutting nearly 150,000 tons in trees over the next 14 months
o Minister announced measures today that are to curb global supply by cutting nearly 150,000 tons in trees over the next 14 months

FARM MINISTER'S MEASURES

Announcing further steps to combat the lowering global price of rubber, the Thai Deputy Farm <u>Minister's measures were announced today for curbing global supply by cutting nearly 150,000 tons in trees over the next 14 months</u>.

- ○ Minister's measures were announced today for curbing global supply by cutting nearly 150,000 tons in trees over the next 14 months
- ○ Minister's measures, which are to curb global supply by cutting nearly 150,000 tons in trees over the next 14 months, were announced today
- ○ Minister's measures for curbing global supply by cutting nearly 150,000 tons in trees over the next 14 months were announced today
- ○ Minister announced measures today to curb global supply by cutting nearly 150,000 tons in trees over the next 14 months
- ○ Minister announced measures today that are to curb global supply by cutting nearly 150,000 tons in trees over the next 14 months

EXPLANATION

Creating a filter: the original sentence uses passive voice unnecessarily. We have identified the Minister; ideally the Minister will do the announcing with active voice.

Applying the filter: our filter limits us to (D) and (E). In (E), the phrase "that are to curb global supply" conveys a meaning that they were commanded to curb global supply, contrary to the intended meaning, which is that the measures are *intended* to curb supply. So (E) is defective, while the infinitive in (D) expresses the intended meaning clearly and simply. The correct answer is (D).

Alongside Petra and the Great Wall of China as one of the seven wonders of the modern world, <u>the Taj Mahal, which was constructed to memorialize Mumtaz Mahal, the third wife of emperor Shah Jahan, after her passing took more than 12 years of thousands of engineers' labor to build</u>.

○   the Taj Mahal, which was constructed to memorialize Mumtaz Mahal, the third wife of emperor Shah Jahan, after her passing took more than 12 years of thousands of engineers' labor to build

○   Mumtaz Mahal, the third wife of emperor Shah Jahan, was memorialized after her passing by the Taj Mahal, which thousands of engineers who labored more than 12 years to build it

○   it took thousands of engineers more than 12 years to build the Taj Mahal to memorialize Mumtaz Mahal, the third wife of emperor Shah Jahan, after her passing

○   thousands of engineers labored more than 12 years to build the Taj Mahal to memorialize Mumtaz Mahal, the third wife of emperor Shah Jahan, after her passing

○   more than 12 years were needed to build the Taj Mahal, which thousands of engineers labored at to memorialize Mumtaz Mahal, the third wife of emperor Shah Jahan, after her passing

THE TAJ MAHAL

Alongside Petra and the Great Wall of China as one of the seven wonders of the modern world, <u>the Taj Mahal, which was constructed to memorialize Mumtaz Mahal, the third wife of emperor Shah Jahan, after her passing took more than 12 years of thousands of engineers' labor to build</u>.

- ○ the Taj Mahal, which was constructed to memorialize Mumtaz Mahal, the third wife of emperor Shah Jahan, after her passing took more than 12 years of thousands of engineers' labor to build
- ○ Mumtaz Mahal, the third wife of emperor Shah Jahan, was memorialized after her passing by the Taj Mahal, which thousands of engineers who labored more than 12 years to build it
- ○ it took thousands of engineers more than 12 years to build the Taj Mahal to memorialize Mumtaz Mahal, the third wife of emperor Shah Jahan, after her passing
- ○ thousands of engineers labored more than 12 years to build the Taj Mahal to memorialize Mumtaz Mahal, the third wife of emperor Shah Jahan, after her passing
- ○ more than 12 years were needed to build the Taj Mahal, which thousands of engineers labored at to memorialize Mumtaz Mahal, the third wife of emperor Shah Jahan, after her passing

EXPLANATION

Creating a filter: the original sentence is a bit confusing. The phrase "after her passing," in particular, is not optimal. The sentence makes it sound like it took more than 12 years to build after her passing, but maybe additional time before her passing, which is probably not the intended meaning of the sentence.

Applying the filter: the answer choices are diverse. They all begin differently. In fact, the beginning of the answer choice comes directly after the modifying phrase that begins with "Alongside Petra..." Nothing other than the Taj Mahal can fit into that slot and be compared with Petra and the Great Wall of China. Answer choice (A) is the only viable option, despite its flaws, because it's the only one without a gross modifier error. The correct answer is (A).

Many people believe that such activities as owning a pet, taking care of another's pet, and, of course, babysitting an infant <u>not only confer the capacity of friendship on a child but also develop</u> role-taking skills, since that child must put him- or herself in the pet or infant's situation and imagine how that pet or infant feels.

○   not only confer the capacity of friendship on a child but also develop

○   confer the capacity of friendship on a child but also are developing

○   are conferring the capacity of friendship on a child but also are developing

○   not only confer the capacity of friendship on a child, they are also developing

○   are conferring the capacity of friendship on a child, and they are also developing

OWNING A PET

Many people believe that such activities as owning a pet, taking care of another's pet, and, of course, babysitting an infant <u>not only confer the capacity of friendship on a child but also develop</u> role-taking skills, since that child must put him- or herself in the pet or infant's situation and imagine how that pet or infant feels.

- O not only confer the capacity of friendship on a child but also develop
- O confer the capacity of friendship on a child but also are developing
- O are conferring the capacity of friendship on a child but also are developing
- O not only confer the capacity of friendship on a child, they are also developing
- O are conferring the capacity of friendship on a child, and they are also developing

EXPLANATION

Creating a filter: the original sentence passes the subject-verb test and has no problematic pronouns. The preposition "on" is correct with the verb "confer"; "confer on" is proper English usage to describe the act of bestowing something, particularly acquired characteristics. We review the answer choices looking for objective defects.

Finding objective defects: choice (B) has a lack of parallelism between "confer" and "developing." That eliminates (B) and (D). Choice (C) uses an ongoing present tense unnecessarily and against the intended sense of the sentence, which describes a generality. Choice (E) has the same problem. The correct answer is (A).

Calling for a ceasefire in South Sudan, where unrest has killed more than a thousand people, China has offered to step forth as the African state's biggest oil investor and <u>act as a peace broker, so that it directly engages</u> both warring sides in order to facilitate negotiations.

- ○ act as a peace broker, so that it directly engages
- ○ act like a peace broker so as to engage directly
- ○ act as a peace broker, directly engaging
- ○ acting as a peace broker, directly engaging
- ○ acting like a peace broker, directly engage

PEACE BROKER

Calling for a ceasefire in South Sudan, where unrest has killed more than a thousand people, China has offered to step forth as the African state's biggest oil investor and <u>act as a peace broker, so that it directly engages</u> both warring sides in order to facilitate negotiations.

- ○ act as a peace broker, so that it directly engages
- ○ act like a peace broker so as to engage directly
- ○ act as a peace broker, directly engaging
- ○ acting as a peace broker, directly engaging
- ○ acting like a peace broker, directly engage

EXPLANATION

Creating a filter: in the original sentence, the phrase "act as a peace broker, so that it directly engages" is redundant in including "so that," since directly engaging is part of what a peace broker will do. So we cut to the answer choices to look for more straightforward wording.

Applying the filter: (C) is good. "Act" must be in parallel form with "step" in "to step forth." Choices (D) and (E) are therefore out. Choice (B) has the same problem as (A), and also incorrectly uses the word "like," which would be appropriate if China *wasn't* a peace broker, contrary to the intended meaning. The correct answer is (C).

Similarities across 200 genes related to hearing and deafness <u>that were discovered in new research have yielded proof of echolocation capabilities in cetaceans, including dolphins, that were evolving independently of but</u> convergent with the sonar hearing capabilities for which bats are well known.

○ that were discovered in new research have yielded proof of echolocation capabilities in cetaceans, including dolphins, that were evolving independently of but

○ that were discovered in new research yields proof of echolocation capabilities in cetaceans, including dolphins, that were evolving independently of but also

○ having been discovered in new research have yielded proof of echolocation capabilities in cetaceans, including dolphins, that were evolving independently of but

○ discovered in new research yields proof of echolocation capabilities in cetaceans, including dolphins, evolving independently but also

○ discovered in new research have yielded proof of echolocation capabilities in cetaceans, including dolphins, that evolved independently of but

Cetacean Echolocation

Similarities across 200 genes related to hearing and deafness <u>that were discovered in new research have yielded proof of echolocation capabilities in cetaceans, including dolphins, that were evolving independently of but</u> convergent with the sonar hearing capabilities for which bats are well known.

- o that were discovered in new research have yielded proof of echolocation capabilities in cetaceans, including dolphins, that were evolving independently of but
- o that were discovered in new research yields proof of echolocation capabilities in cetaceans, including dolphins, that were evolving independently of but also
- o having been discovered in new research have yielded proof of echolocation capabilities in cetaceans, including dolphins, that were evolving independently of but
- o discovered in new research yields proof of echolocation capabilities in cetaceans, including dolphins, evolving independently but also
- o discovered in new research have yielded proof of echolocation capabilities in cetaceans, including dolphins, that evolved independently of but

Explanation

Creating a filter: supposing that we can't find a defect in the original sentence, we can head to the answer choices.

Finding objective defects: choices (D) and (E) begin in a more succinct manner than (A) and (B), and they are equally clear. Choices (D) and (E) also allow us to avoid using "that were" twice in the sentence, which was creating awkwardness. So (A) and (B) are out. Answer choice (C) uses the more elaborate "having been discovered" without need. So (C) is out and we focus on (D) and (E). There are number of differences between them. One difference will do the trick if we are fully confident in it. "New research" indicates that something has happened recently, and for that "have yielded" in (E) is accurate. "Yields" would imply what we are talking about is generally the case, contrary to what's implied by the phrase "new research." The correct answer is (E).

Looking at search engine trends, <u>evidence has been gathered by reporters indicating that, despite recent actions making the practice illegal, American interest in unlocking cell phones is much higher than they had</u> previously thought.

○   evidence has been gathered by reporters indicating that, despite recent actions making the practice illegal, American interest in unlocking cell phones is much higher than they had

○   evidence has been gathered by reporters indicating, despite recent actions making the practice illegal, a much higher American interest in unlocking cell phones than had been

○   reporters have gathered evidence indicating that, despite recent actions making the practice illegal, American interest in unlocking cell phones is much higher than

○   reporters have gathered evidence that indicates, despite recent actions making the practice illegal, a much higher American interest in unlocking cell phones than that which was

○   reporters have gathered evidence which indicates, despite recent actions making the practice illegal, a much higher American interest in unlocking cell phones than that

UNLOCKING CELL PHONES

Looking at search engine trends, <u>evidence has been gathered by reporters indicating that, despite recent actions making the practice illegal, American interest in unlocking cell phones is much higher than they had</u> previously thought.

- ○ evidence has been gathered by reporters indicating that, despite recent actions making the practice illegal, American interest in unlocking cell phones is much higher than they had
- ○ evidence has been gathered by reporters indicating, despite recent actions making the practice illegal, a much higher American interest in unlocking cell phones than had been
- ○ reporters have gathered evidence indicating that, despite recent actions making the practice illegal, American interest in unlocking cell phones is much higher than
- ○ reporters have gathered evidence that indicates, despite recent actions making the practice illegal, a much higher American interest in unlocking cell phones than that which was
- ○ reporters have gathered evidence which indicates, despite recent actions making the practice illegal, a much higher American interest in unlocking cell phones than that

EXPLANATION

Creating a filter: the initial phrase "looking at search engine trends" grammatically modifies "evidence," but that's not the intended meaning; the evidence is not doing the looking. We cut to the answer choices for options that begin with a noun that can perform the act of looking.

Applying the filter: our filter leaves us with choices (C) through (E). The *reporters* found something. That finding is expressed in a statement, so we're going to look for the word "that" to introduce that indirect statement. (C) has it, and (D) and (E) do not. Moreover, choices (D) and (E) have other problems; one of them is that the "despite recent actions" modifier is now ambiguous and could actually refer to the manner in which the evidence does its indicating. The correct answer is (C).

The top five rubber-producing countries are fairly geographically concentrated around and <u>include Malaysia, which can produce up to 1 million metric tons of rubber annually and is</u> famous for the forests of Borneo.

○ include Malaysia, which can produce up to 1 million metric tons of rubber annually and is
○ include Malaysia, producing so much as 1 million metric tons of rubber annually and
○ include Malaysia, producing up to 1 million metric tons of rubber annually and being
○ includes Malaysia, which can produce so much as 1 million metric tons of rubber annually and is
○ includes Malaysia, which can produce up to 1 million metric tons of rubber annually and it is

RUBBER PRODUCERS

The top five rubber-producing countries are fairly geographically concentrated around and <u>include Malaysia, which can produce up to 1 million metric tons of rubber annually and is</u> famous for the forests of Borneo.

o   include Malaysia, which can produce up to 1 million metric tons of rubber annually and is
o   include Malaysia, producing so much as 1 million metric tons of rubber annually and
o   include Malaysia, producing up to 1 million metric tons of rubber annually and being
o   includes Malaysia, which can produce so much as 1 million metric tons of rubber annually and is
o   includes Malaysia, which can produce up to 1 million metric tons of rubber annually and it is

EXPLANATION

Creating a filter: supposing we can't find an error, we look to the answer choices.

Finding objective defects: we see a 3 versus 2 standoff between "include" and "includes." The grammatical subject is "countries," so the verb must be "include," limiting us to (A) through (C). Choice (C) uses the gerund "being" unnecessarily and (B) uses an improper idiom, "so much as," which would be "as much as" when used properly. The correct answer is (A).

In the Amazon, the alignment of a fertile ecosystem and <u>isolation from other ecologies during early geological epochs has given rise to a great diversity of species, which, in many genuses, outnumber</u> those in other regions on Earth by 100 to 1.

- ○ isolation from other ecologies during early geological epochs has given rise to a great diversity of species, which, in many genuses, outnumber
- ○ isolation from other ecologies during early geological epochs has given rise to a great diversity of species, which, in many genuses, outnumbered
- ○ of isolation from other ecologies during early geological epochs have given rise to a great diversity of species that, in many genuses, outnumbered
- ○ of both isolation from other ecologies during early geological epochs have given rise to a great diversity of species that, in many genuses, outnumber
- ○ of isolation from other ecologies during early geological epochs has given rise to a great diversity of species that has, in many genuses, been outnumbering

AMAZONIAN DIVERSITY

In the Amazon, the alignment of a fertile ecosystem and <u>isolation from other ecologies during early geological epochs has given rise to a great diversity of species, which, in many genuses, outnumber</u> those in other regions on Earth by 100 to 1.

○ isolation from other ecologies during early geological epochs has given rise to a great diversity of species, which, in many genuses, outnumber

○ isolation from other ecologies during early geological epochs has given rise to a great diversity of species, which, in many genuses, outnumbered

○ of isolation from other ecologies during early geological epochs have given rise to a great diversity of species that, in many genuses, outnumbered

○ of both isolation from other ecologies during early geological epochs have given rise to a great diversity of species that, in many genuses, outnumber

○ of isolation from other ecologies during early geological epochs has given rise to a great diversity of species that has, in many genuses, been outnumbering

EXPLANATION

Creating a filter: when we read the sentence as written, an error may not leap out, so we can examine the answer choices.

Finding objective defects: we see a 2 versus 3 standoff between using the word "of" and not using "of" at the beginning of the answer. Checking back, both appear to be allowed by the sentence. So we look for more objective grounds to rule out answer choices. We have a lot of verb differences. "Has given" should be grammatically singular, since its grammatical subject is the singular "alignment." Ecosystem and isolation are nouns, but not subjects of the sentence, because they are locked within the prepositional phrase starting with "of." That rules out (C) and (D), which both use "have given." Then there's "outnumber." We are describing a generality, so the simple present tense is appropriate. That rules out (B) and (E). The correct answer is (A).

V. important

Redo

tense
singular/plural

Although their primary attempt for business expansion would take place in the Indian market, manufacturers of low-cost cell phones could not afford to sacrifice the price-sensitive segment of developed markets because <u>if they gave that up, their footing to enter India was forever shaky</u>.

- ○ if they gave that up, their footing to enter India was forever shaky
- ○ without it their footing to enter India would be forever shaky
- ○ their footing to enter India was forever shaky if they gave that up
- ○ without that, they would be forever shaky about their footing to enter India
- ○ forever would their footing to enter India be shaky if they gave that up

FOOTING IN INDIA

Although their primary attempt for business expansion would take place in the Indian market, manufacturers of low-cost cell phones could not afford to sacrifice the price-sensitive segment of developed markets because <u>if they gave that up, their footing to enter India was forever shaky</u>.

- ○ if they gave that up, their footing to enter India was forever shaky
- ○ without it their footing to enter India would be forever shaky
- ○ their footing to enter India was forever shaky if they gave that up
- ○ without that, they would be forever shaky about their footing to enter India
- ○ forever would their footing to enter India be shaky if they gave that up

EXPLANATION

Creating a filter: in this question, in the underlined portion, something is off with the verb "was." We are talking about what would prevail in the past under a condition specified by the word "if," so we need the conditional tense – we need a "would" word. In other words, "*if* they had given that up, they *would* have been doomed." We go to the answer choices in search of the conditional tense.

Applying the filter: (B), (D), and (E) have the conditional tense we are looking for.

Finding objective defects: choice (D) conveys a sense contrary to the intended meaning. *They* aren't shaky – like, scared or something – their footing is. The word order in (E) is inferior; the word "shaky" is far from "footing" and far from "forever," and it wants to be close to words it's related to. In (E), moreover, the word "that" at the end is far from its referent. Choice (B) is clearer and better English idiom. The correct answer is (B).

In a "smart home," home security systems, heating units, televisions, and washing machines are all networked, and the homeowner can send commands by phone to each <u>appliance, which thereby activates or deactivates</u> that unit as desired.

- ○ appliance, which thereby activates or deactivates
- ○ appliance, in turn activating or deactivating
- ○ appliance, and it will activate or deactivate
- ○ appliance and thereby activate or deactivate
- ○ appliance which, as a result, activates or deactivates

SMART HOMES

In a "smart home," home security systems, heating units, televisions, and washing machines are all networked, and the homeowner can send commands by phone to each <u>appliance, which thereby activates or deactivates</u> that unit as desired.

- ○ appliance, which thereby activates or deactivates
- ○ appliance, in turn activating or deactivating
- ○ appliance, and it will activate or deactivate
- ○ appliance and thereby activate or deactivate
- ○ appliance which, as a result, activates or deactivates

EXPLANATION

Creating a filter: the original sentence has an issue with the relative pronoun "which." It grammatically modifies "appliance," but that's not the intended meaning; the commands do the activating, not the appliance. Choice (A) is out. We'll look for an answer choice that corrects the error.

Applying the filter: choice (B) is defective because the phrase "in turn" indicates that the thing is shutting on and off according to some logic or sequence, whereas the intended meaning is on *or* off according to the each command. Choice (C) has a bad pronoun. Choice (D) uses the suspicious thereby but does so correctly. Choice (E) is defective because the verb "activates" is grammatically singular and meant to go with the grammatical subject "commands." The correct answer is (D).

A new law proposed by privacy advocates <u>would increase the amount of tint that carmakers have been allowed to build</u> into the windows of their vehicles.

- ○ would increase the amount of tint that carmakers have been allowed to build
- ○ would increase the tint amount that carmakers have been building
- ○ will increase the tint amount carmakers are allowed to build
- ○ would increase the amount of tint that carmakers are allowed to build
- ○ will increase the amount of tint allowed for windows by carmakers

TINTED WINDOWS

A new law proposed by privacy advocates <u>would increase the amount of tint that carmakers have been allowed to build</u> into the windows of their vehicles.

- ○ would increase the amount of tint that carmakers have been allowed to build
- ○ would increase the tint amount that carmakers have been building
- ○ will increase the tint amount carmakers are allowed to build
- ○ would increase the amount of tint that carmakers are allowed to build
- ○ will increase the amount of tint allowed for windows by carmakers

EXPLANATION

Creating a filter: in the original sentence, the conditional tense in "would increase" is appropriate; the law isn't in effect yet, so the effect is expressed in the conditional tense. However, the verb tense in the phrase "have been allowed to build" isn't correct; it indicates, contrary to the intended meaning, that the law is changing what carmakers were allowed to do *in the recent past*.

Applying the filter: choice (B) has the same problem. Choices (C) and (E) fail to use "would." Could such the indicative (normal) verb tense be correct here? It could be a reasonable intended meaning of a sentence similar to this one that the bill *will* pass with certainty and the effect *will* take place. However, we can infer that the intended meaning of the sentence in this question is different, because it refers to a "proposed" law. The law, evidently, will not necessarily pass, so the intended meaning is conveyed by the conditional tense, not by the indicative tense. Furthermore, (C) uses the unidiomatic "tint amount," while (E) uses the unidiomatic "allowed for windows by carmakers." The correct answer is (D).

Investigations along the Solo river in Indonesia have led some archeologists to debunk the idea of an era <u>in which Homo Erectus had still survived in then Homo Sapiens' inhabited areas</u>.

- ○ in which Homo Erectus had still survived in then Homo Sapiens' inhabited areas
- ○ in which Homo Erectus still survived in areas inhabited by Homo Sapiens
- ○ when Homo Erectus still survived where there were areas inhabited by Homo Sapiens
- ○ when Homo Erectus had still survived in current Homo Sapiens areas
- ○ when Homo Erectus still survived in areas that were then Homo Sapiens'

THE SOLO RIVER

Investigations along the Solo river in Indonesia have led some archeologists to debunk the idea of an era <u>in which Homo Erectus had still survived in then Homo Sapiens' inhabited areas</u>.

- o in which Homo Erectus had still survived in then Homo Sapiens' inhabited areas
- o in which Homo Erectus still survived in areas inhabited by Homo Sapiens
- o when Homo Erectus still survived where there were areas inhabited by Homo Sapiens
- o when Homo Erectus had still survived in current Homo Sapiens areas
- o when Homo Erectus still survived in areas that were then Homo Sapiens'

EXPLANATION

Creating a filter: in this question, the construction "in which" may stand out. The answer choices show that "in which" and "when" are alternatives we must choose between. Both phrases, "in which" and "when," convey meaning accurately here. More of a problem is the phrase "in then Homo Sapiens' inhabited areas," an awkward string of words.

Applying the filter: (B) looks better and clear. Choice (C) has strange phrasing that leaves us uncertain whether the two groups are in the same area, as the sentence intends to say. Choice (D) has the same problem as (A). Choice (E) distorts the meaning of the sentence; the intended meaning isn't that any areas *belonged* to Homo Sapiens; we're talking about cohabitation. The correct answer is (B).

Despite its being soft enough to grow, a newborn human has a skull that is not an unbroken casing with "soft spots," rather it is a series of body plates joined together by anatomical lines known as sutures.

- Despite its being soft enough to grow, a newborn human has a skull that is not an unbroken casing with "soft spots," rather it is
- Despite being soft enough to grow, a newborn human's skull is not an unbroken casing with "soft spots," but is
- Despite being soft enough to grow, a newborn human's skull is not an unbroken casing nor does it have "soft spots," but rather
- Although soft enough to grow, a newborn human's skull is not an unbroken casing with "soft spots," but rather
- Although soft enough to grow, a newborn human's skull is not an unbroken casing with "soft spots," but

SOFT SKULLS

Despite its being soft enough to grow, a newborn human has a skull that is not an unbroken casing with "soft spots," rather it is a series of body plates joined together by anatomical lines known as sutures.

- ○ Despite its being soft enough to grow, a newborn human has a skull that is not an unbroken casing with "soft spots," rather it is
- ○ Despite being soft enough to grow, a newborn human's skull is not an unbroken casing with "soft spots," but is
- ○ Despite being soft enough to grow, a newborn human's skull is not an unbroken casing nor does it have "soft spots," but rather
- ○ Although soft enough to grow, a newborn human's skull is not an unbroken casing with "soft spots," but rather
- ○ Although soft enough to grow, a newborn human's skull is not an unbroken casing with "soft spots," but

EXPLANATION

Creating a filter: in the original sentence, the phrase "despite its being soft enough to grow" grammatically modifies "human," and that's not the intended meaning. The skull of the newborn is what's soft, according to the intended meaning. We eliminate (A) and go straight to the other answer choices to eliminate others with modification errors.

Applying the filter: as it turns out, (B) through (E) are all free of the error in (A). So we'll move straight to finding defects in the other choices.

Finding objective defects: choices (B) and (C) use the gerund unnecessarily in the phrase "despite being," so we focus on (D) and (E), which end differently. The phrase "but rather" is clear in this case, in which we are saying the baby's skull is *not* one thing, *but rather* another. Since the word "but" alone can mean different things, we prefer to use "but rather" when relevant for clear meaning, though it's not an absolute requirement. Choice (E) is scarcely flawed, but (D) is objectively clearer and still succinct. The correct answer is (D).

During medieval times, Augustine monks in Scotland favored using watercress as a means <u>to combat scurvy and administering</u> hemlock as a painkiller, revealing a detailed knowledge of the medicinal properties of herbs.

- ○ to combat scurvy and administering
- ○ to combat scurvy and to administer
- ○ of combating scurvy and of administering
- ○ of combating scurvy and administer
- ○ for combating scurvy and the administration of

MEDICINAL MONKS

During medieval times, Augustine monks in Scotland favored using watercress as a means <u>to combat scurvy and administering</u> hemlock as a painkiller, revealing a detailed knowledge of the medicinal properties of herbs.

- ○ to combat scurvy and administering
- ○ to combat scurvy and to administer
- ○ of combating scurvy and of administering
- ○ of combating scurvy and administer
- ○ for combating scurvy and the administration of

EXPLANATION

Creating a filter: in this sentence, there is a potential parallelism issue between "combat" and "administering." Should "administering" be "administer"? The intended meaning of the sentence will be the judge. We look closer at what it's trying to say. We're talking about a use of watercress and a different use hemlock. "Administering" is parallel with "using," and therefore is correct. That means that (A) might be right, so far, and we can take our observation to filter the other answer choices.

Applying the filter: based on our decision about (A), choices (B), (D), and (E) are defective. In (C), "administering" looks like it's parallel with "using," but it's preceded by "of" and therefore grammatically under the jurisdiction of "combating," which is contrary to the intended meaning. So (C) is wrong. That leaves (A) as the correct answer. We didn't have to worry about whether the "to combat" or "of combating" was better here, but the answer to that is that, when we are talking about a verb, the infinitive will be superior, whereas a preposition such as "of" is best used with a true noun, not a gerund. The correct answer is (A).

Using a 64-beam laser to create a detailed 3D map of its environment, the self-driving car prototype, although already obsolete, <u>proved as equipped for navigating any conditions roads could put in front of it</u>.

○   proved as equipped for navigating any conditions roads could put in front of it
○   proved itself equipped to navigate any conditions roads could put in front of it
○   proved as equipped to navigate any conditions roads could put in front of it
○   prove to be as equipped to navigate any conditions roads could put in front of it
○   proved to have been equipped for navigating any conditions roads could put in front of it

CAR PROTOTYPE

Using a 64-beam laser to create a detailed 3D map of its environment, the self-driving car prototype, although already obsolete, <u>proved as equipped for navigating any conditions roads could put in front of it</u>.

○   proved as equipped for navigating any conditions roads could put in front of it
○   proved itself equipped to navigate any conditions roads could put in front of it
○   proved as equipped to navigate any conditions roads could put in front of it
○   prove to be as equipped to navigate any conditions roads could put in front of it
○   proved to have been equipped for navigating any conditions roads could put in front of it

EXPLANATION

Creating a filter: the original sentence is defective, since the comparative "as" always properly comes in pairs; the prototype must be *as* equipped *as* something else for the word to be used right.

Applying the filter: we eliminate choices (A) and (C). And also choice (D), for that matter: there's a sneaky "as" after "to be." We're left with (B) and (E). Choice (E)'s verb tense is unnecessarily complex; it appears to refer to some other time in the past that isn't mentioned in the sentence. The correct answer is (B).

According to one biographer, Steve Jobs' passion for the details of music, philosophy and <u>other fields in the humanities were critical to his success, influencing his sense of design as much as</u> his technological savvy did.

○   those other fields in the humanities were critical to his success, influencing his sense of design as much as

○   those other fields in the humanities was critical to his success, and it influenced his sense of design as well as

○   other fields in the humanities was critical to his success, influencing his sense of design as much as

○   other fields in the humanities was critical to his success, as it influenced his sense of design as much as

○   other fields in the humanities were critical to his success, influencing both his sense of design in addition to that which

According to one biographer, Steve Jobs' passion for the details of music, philosophy and <u>other fields in the humanities were critical to his success, influencing his sense of design as much as</u> his technological savvy did.

○   those other fields in the humanities were critical to his success, influencing his sense of design as much as

○   those other fields in the humanities was critical to his success, and it influenced his sense of design as well as

○   other fields in the humanities was critical to his success, influencing his sense of design as much as

○   other fields in the humanities was critical to his success, as it influenced his sense of design as much as

○   other fields in the humanities were critical to his success, influencing both his sense of design in addition to that which

EXPLANATION

Creating a filter: the original sentence has a verb error. The grammatical subject corresponding to the verb "were" is "passion," which is grammatically singular. "Music," "philosophy," and "fields" are nouns but are within the prepositional phrase beginning with "of," so they cannot be the grammatical subject. We can start by filtering on that error.

Applying the filter: based on the filter, we eliminate (A) and (E). We'll narrow down (B), (C) and (D) on other grounds.

Finding objective defects: choice (B) uses the phrase "as well as," and that phrase doesn't convey the intended meaning correctly. The "as well as" doesn't fit because, idiomatically, we describe influence in terms of degree or amount (how much it influenced) and in terms of quality (whether it did a good job of influencing). Choice (D) is grammatically legal but distorts the intended meaning. Without the word "as," the latter phrase is descriptive. With the "as," it's giving a reason. So it seems to be saying, "Why was Jobs' passion for humanities critical to his success? Because it influenced his design the same amount as his technological savvy did." That's sensible but off base, because in the intended sense the latter portion is an elaboration of the main point, not a condition for it. The correct answer is (C).

Assuming that the new drug is approved, it will remain to be seen <u>whether it decreases post-traumatic stress disorder in military veterans after it is widely administered</u>.

- whether it decreases post-traumatic stress disorder in military veterans after it is widely administered
- whether it decreases post-traumatic stress disorder in military veterans once they widely administer it
- whether it decreases post-traumatic stress disorder in military veterans once it has been widely administered
- if it decreases post-traumatic stress disorder in military veterans once it is widely administered
- if it decreases post-traumatic stress disorder in military veterans after it has been widely administered

STRESS DRUG

Assuming that the new drug is approved, it will remain to be seen <u>whether it decreases post-traumatic stress disorder in military veterans after it is widely administered</u>.

○ whether it decreases post-traumatic stress disorder in military veterans after it is widely administered

○ whether it decreases post-traumatic stress disorder in military veterans once they widely administer it

○ whether it decreases post-traumatic stress disorder in military veterans once it has been widely administered

○ if it decreases post-traumatic stress disorder in military veterans once it is widely administered

○ if it decreases post-traumatic stress disorder in military veterans after it has been widely administered

EXPLANATION

Creating a filter: We read the sentence and, drifting to the answer choices, see a 3 versus 2 standoff of "whether" against "if." This is a yes-or-no question, not a condition, so "whether" is correct and "if" is incorrect. We'll filter for choices that use "whether."

Applying the filter: our filter leaves us with (A) through (C).

Finding objective defects: choice (B) introduces an ambiguous pronoun "they," which seems to indicate that veterans are administering the drug, contrary to intended meaning. Choices (A) and (C) are similar. Which conveys the intended meaning? We can see that (A) is imprecise and (C) is precise. Contrary to the intended meaning, (A) makes it sound as if we might be wondering whether the new drug will have an effect *before* it's administered, or during its administration. The administration is meant to be the precondition for the intended effect. The word "once" and the verb tense "has been" both do that accurately. Here the present perfect verb "has been administered" is fitting, because we want to convey that the administration occurs right before the effect will or will not be seen. The correct answer is (C).

First-year sales of the <u>film *Bridge on the River Kwai* obtained in 1957, and estimated to be 27 million dollars, made it the largest-grossing movie</u> of the year.

○ film *Bridge on the River Kwai* obtained in 1957, and estimated to be 27 million dollars, made it the largest-grossing movie

○ film *Bridge on the River Kwai,* that they obtained in 1957, had been estimated to be 27 million dollars, thus making it the largest-grossing movie

○ film *Bridge on the River Kwai* that were obtained in 1957, were estimated to be 27 million dollars, making this the largest-grossing movie

○ film *Bridge on the River Kwai,* obtained in 1957, were estimated to be 27 million dollars, making it the largest-grossing movie

○ film *Bridge on the River Kwai* which, obtained in 1957, were estimated to be 27 million dollars, made it the largest-grossing movie

First-year sales of the <u>film *Bridge on the River Kwai* obtained in 1957, and estimated to be 27 million dollars, made it the largest-grossing movie</u> of the year.

- film *Bridge on the River Kwai* obtained in 1957, and estimated to be 27 million dollars, made it the largest-grossing movie
- film *Bridge on the River Kwai,* that they obtained in 1957, had been estimated to be 27 million dollars, thus making it the largest-grossing movie
- film *Bridge on the River Kwai* that were obtained in 1957, were estimated to be 27 million dollars, making this the largest-grossing movie
- film *Bridge on the River Kwai,* obtained in 1957, were estimated to be 27 million dollars, making it the largest-grossing movie
- film *Bridge on the River Kwai* which, obtained in 1957, were estimated to be 27 million dollars, made it the largest-grossing movie

EXPLANATION

Creating a filter: the original sentence has defects. The phrase, "and estimated to be 27 million dollars" is set off by commas, but it's not a modifier, because it has the conjunction "and." Furthermore, the phrase can't be an independent clause, because it has no grammatical subject. **A grammatical subject and its predicate may not be spliced by a single comma (such an error is called a "comma splice").**

Applying the filter: We eliminate (A) and scan and see answer choice (C) has the same problem. We'll look for other grounds to eliminate further.

Finding objective defects: the other answer choices insert commas in an attempt to make the 1957 part into a legitimate modifier. Choice (B) introduces a pronoun with no reference, "they," so it's out. Answer choice (D) sounds good. Answer choice (E) is not grammatical. The relative pronoun "which" would have to be preceded by a comma here, since we have already defined what we are talking about and the modifier is only providing bonus information. Furthermore, it's awkward with a modifier inside a modifier. The correct answer is (D).

The best way to install good habits in a dog is <u>to condition it with short verbal commands and edible rewards before they solidify bad habits when aging takes effect</u>.

- to condition it with short verbal commands and edible rewards before they solidify bad habits when aging takes effect
- if they are conditioned with short verbal commands and edible rewards before aging solidifies their bad habits
- for it to be conditioned with short verbal commands and edible rewards before aging takes effect and solidifies bad habits
- if the dog is conditioned with short verbal commands and edible rewards before they solidify bad habits when aging takes effect
- to have it conditioned with short verbal commands and edible rewards before aging takes effect and solidifies bad habits

DOG HABITS

The best way to install good habits in a dog is <u>to condition it with short verbal commands and edible rewards before they solidify bad habits when aging takes effect</u>.

- ○ to condition it with short verbal commands and edible rewards before they solidify bad habits when aging takes effect
- ○ if they are conditioned with short verbal commands and edible rewards before aging solidifies their bad habits
- ○ for it to be conditioned with short verbal commands and edible rewards before aging takes effect and solidifies bad habits
- ○ if the dog is conditioned with short verbal commands and edible rewards before they solidify bad habits when aging takes effect
- ○ to have it conditioned with short verbal commands and edible rewards before aging takes effect and solidifies bad habits

EXPLANATION

Creating a filter: In the original sentence here, there may be more than one problem, but we can fixate on the use of grammatically singular "dog" early in the sentence and grammatically plural pronoun "they" later on.

Applying the filter: our filter eliminates choices (A), (B) and (D).

Finding objective defects: we compare how (C) and (E) begin. Choice (C) is idiomatically poor, and moreover the beginning of the sentence should be parallel with "to install," because the linking verb "is" equates the grammatical subject and predicate of the sentence. The correct answer is (E).

Offering a suite of similar products at dissimilar prices is critical to ongoing profitability for the automotive industry, <u>like in other industries</u>.

- ○ like in other industries
- ○ as in other industries
- ○ just as it is in other industries
- ○ as other industries do
- ○ as it is for other industries

PRODUCT SUITE

Offering a suite of similar products at dissimilar prices is critical to ongoing profitability for the automotive industry, <u>like in other industries</u>.

- ○ like in other industries
- ○ as in other industries
- ○ just as it is in other industries
- ○ as other industries do
- ○ as it is for other industries

EXPLANATION

Creating a filter: we have a comparison in the original sentence, as is signaled by the word "like," so we must examine it. In general, the word "like" most exactly is employed to compare things and their characteristics, while the word "as" compares how things are done. In this sentence, the proper usage is the word "as," because we are not comparing the characteristics of things, but rather the *way* a suite of similar products is critical in both one industry and others.

Applying the filter: we are left with all answer choices other than (A). All the other answer choices use "as." One difference among them is their treatment of prepositions. **Often in Sentence Correction questions, one preposition is required over another not because of general usage rules, but because parallelism in the sentence requires the use of a particular pronoun.** In other words, we must not stare at the answer choices and keep repeating "in other industries" and "for other industries" in our mind's ear, wondering which is better in isolation. Rather, the best one is determined by parallelism with the prior part of the sentence. Namely, the product suite is critical *for* the automotive industry as it is *for* other industries. Answer choice (E), therefore, is the only valid option. If we were to write this sentence, we might have reasons to use the preposition "in," but without being able to change the non-underlined portion of the sentence, that option is barred to us here. The correct answer is (E).

That Buddha was born earlier than previously had been thought is not exactly proved by the recent discovery of a Buddhist shrine, but <u>in ascribing design elements of the shrine to a factor other than an earlier existence of Buddha,</u> the man's influence will have to be reconsidered.

- ○ in ascribing design elements of the shrine to a factor other than an earlier existence of Buddha,
- ○ if the elements of the shrine's design are ascribed to a factor other than an earlier existence of Buddha,
- ○ in ascribing elements of the shrine's design to a factor other than an earlier existence of Buddha,
- ○ if a factor other than an earlier existence of Buddha is ascribed as the factor of the elements of the shrine's design
- ○ in ascribing something other than an earlier existence of Buddha to the elements of the shrine's design

BUDDHA'S BIRTH

That Buddha was born earlier than previously had been thought is not exactly proved by the recent discovery of a Buddhist shrine, but <u>in ascribing design elements of the shrine to a factor other than an earlier existence of Buddha,</u> the man's influence will have to be reconsidered.

- o in ascribing design elements of the shrine to a factor other than an earlier existence of Buddha,
- o if the elements of the shrine's design are ascribed to a factor other than an earlier existence of Buddha,
- o in ascribing elements of the shrine's design to a factor other than an earlier existence of Buddha,
- o if a factor other than an earlier existence of Buddha is ascribed as the factor of the elements of the shrine's design
- o in ascribing something other than an earlier existence of Buddha to the elements of the shrine's design

EXPLANATION

Creating a filter: the grammar of the original sentence conveys something contrary to its intended meaning. As written, the sentence says nonsensically that the man's influence was the thing ascribing design elements. The defect is due to the fact that the phrase "in ascribing..." modifies "influence."

Applying the filter: answer choices (C) and (E) have the same defect as (A), so they also are eliminated. Choice (B) fixes the error by removing the modifying phrase (and replacing it with a complete clause). We have passive voice, but there's a reason in this case: the ascribing is happening in general and/or by unidentified parties. Answer choice (D) uses the verb "ascribed" incorrectly; the proper usage is "ascribed to," which is similar to "attributed to." The correct answer is (B).

Arguably, the Charles Dickens' current popular fame is <u>not owed to *A Tale of Two Cities,* or *Great Expectations,* but</u> *A Christmas Carol,* thanks to the many TV and movie adaptations of that story.

- ○ not owed to *A Tale of Two Cities*, or Great Expectations, but
- ○ not owed to *A Tale of Two Cities*, or Great Expectations, but is to
- ○ owed not to *A Tale of Two Cities*, or Great Expectations, but to
- ○ owed not to *A Tale of Two Cities*, or Great Expectations, but
- ○ owed not to *A Tale of Two Cities*, or Great Expectations, but is to

A CHRISTMAS CAROL

Arguably, the Charles Dickens' current popular fame is <u>not owed to *A Tale of Two Cities,* or *Great Expectations,* but</u> *A Christmas Carol,* thanks to the many TV and movie adaptations of that story.

o   not owed to *A Tale of Two Cities*, or Great Expectations, but
o   not owed to *A Tale of Two Cities*, or Great Expectations, but is to
o   owed not to *A Tale of Two Cities*, or Great Expectations, but to
o   owed not to *A Tale of Two Cities*, or Great Expectations, but
o   owed not to *A Tale of Two Cities*, or Great Expectations, but is to

EXPLANATION

Creating a filter: in this question, the words "not owed" are in the wrong order. The fame is indeed owed to something; what we are negating is what it's owed to, and so the "not" should come after the verb and modify *Two Cities*.

Applying the filter: we eliminate (B) also, so we're left with (C) through (E).

Finding objective defects: parallelism further dictates that (C) is the correct answer. The fame is owed *to* the book *A Christmas Carol*. Note also that including a verb such as "is," as (B) and (E) do, creates an ungrammatical structure, a phrase with a conjunction and a verb but no grammatical subject. The correct answer is (C).

Since the 1970s, scientists have believed that <u>an asteroid once landed in the Gulf of Mexico and released ash causing a darkening of the sky by 10 to 20 percent over the ensuing decade, which inhibited photosynthesis and leading</u> to the extinction of countless species on Earth.

- ○ an asteroid once landed in the Gulf of Mexico and released ash causing a darkening of the sky by 10 to 20 percent over the ensuing decade, which inhibited photosynthesis and leading
- ○ an asteroid once landed in the Gulf of Mexico and that released ash was what caused a darkening of the sky by 10 to 20 percent over the ensuing decade, and it inhibited photosynthesis and led
- ○ an asteroid once landed in the Gulf of Mexico and released ash causing a darkening of the sky by 10 to 20 percent over the ensuing decade, inhibiting photosynthesis and leading
- ○ a darkening of the sky by 10 to 20 percent caused by the released ash over the ensuing decade after an asteroid once landed in the Gulf of Mexico, inhibited photosynthesis and it led
- ○ a darkening of the sky by 10 to 20 percent caused by the released ash over the ensuing decade after an asteroid once landed in the Gulf of Mexico, inhibiting photosynthesis and it led

GULF ASTEROID

Since the 1970s, scientists have believed that <u>an asteroid once landed in the Gulf of Mexico and released ash causing a darkening of the sky by 10 to 20 percent over the ensuing decade, which inhibited photosynthesis and leading</u> to the extinction of countless species on Earth.

- an asteroid once landed in the Gulf of Mexico and released ash causing a darkening of the sky by 10 to 20 percent over the ensuing decade, which inhibited photosynthesis and leading
- an asteroid once landed in the Gulf of Mexico and that released ash was what caused a darkening of the sky by 10 to 20 percent over the ensuing decade, and it inhibited photosynthesis and led
- an asteroid once landed in the Gulf of Mexico and released ash causing a darkening of the sky by 10 to 20 percent over the ensuing decade, inhibiting photosynthesis and leading
- a darkening of the sky by 10 to 20 percent caused by the released ash over the ensuing decade after an asteroid once landed in the Gulf of Mexico, inhibited photosynthesis and it led
- a darkening of the sky by 10 to 20 percent caused by the released ash over the ensuing decade after an asteroid once landed in the Gulf of Mexico, inhibiting photosynthesis and it led

EXPLANATION

Creating a filter: In this question, the original sentence has an error at the end of the underlined portion: "leading" should be the past tense verb "led" in order to be parallel with "inhibited."

Applying the filter: as we look at the answer choices after (A), we can focus first on the latter two verbs. Choice (B) fixes the problem with "led" but makes other changes; it replaces "which" with a phrase with the pronoun "it," which has ambiguous reference, so (B) is out. Choice (C) has parallel verbs with "inhibiting" and "leading," so it passes our filter. Choice (D) creates an ungrammatical structure in which "inhibited," in coming after a comma splice, has no grammatical verb, so (D) is out. Choice (E) is not parallel between "inhibiting" and "led." The correct answer is (C).

Aggressive cost-cutting campaigns have shown promise in the company's publishing division, the home to a few new startups <u>that have grown at the same pace as the startups</u> disrupting the industry through free journalism and user-submitted articles.

- ○ that have grown at the same pace as the startups
- ○ that will have grown at the same pace as have the startups
- ○ that have grown at the same pace as had those startups
- ○ growing at the same pace as those did
- ○ growing at the same pace as those were

PUBLISHING DIVISION

Aggressive cost-cutting campaigns have shown promise in the company's publishing division, the home to a few new startups <u>that have grown at the same pace as the startups</u> disrupting the industry through free journalism and user-submitted articles.

- ○ that have grown at the same pace as the startups
- ○ that will have grown at the same pace as have the startups
- ○ that have grown at the same pace as had those startups
- ○ growing at the same pace as those did
- ○ growing at the same pace as those were

EXPLANATION

Creating a filter: the original sentence may sound a little funny but not be obviously in error. So we go to answer choice (B), ready to eliminate.

Finding objective defects: choice (B) is contrary to the sentence's intended meaning. In the meaning of the sentence, the campaigns have already shown promise, so the use of the future tense in (B) is not appropriate. Choice (C) has a similar problem: the final modifying phrase, with the word "disrupting," indicates that the intended meaning of this sentence is that startups are *currently* disrupting the industry, so the past perfect tense in the answer choice, "as had those startups," is contrary to intended meaning. Choice (C) is therefore out. Moreover, (D) and (E) have the same past/present mismatch, and are therefore out. We've eliminated all but one choice. The correct answer is (A).

In the 1990s, <u>Australian vineyards, innovators in marketing and in product development, stormed the market with wines both accessible</u> to the palate and psychology of young wine drinkers, and they did so without sacrificing the country's reputation to create vintages of high quality.

o   Australian vineyards, innovators in marketing and in product development, stormed the market with wines both accessible

o   Australian vineyards, innovators in marketing and in product development, stormed the market with wines that were accessible both

o   Australian vineyards, innovators in marketing and in product development, stormed the market with wines accessible

o   innovators in marketing and in product development, Australian vineyards, which stormed the market with wines accessible

o   innovators in marketing and in product development such as Australian vineyards stormed the market with wines accessible both

AUSTRALIAN VINEYARDS

In the 1990s, <u>Australian vineyards, innovators in marketing and in product development, stormed the market with wines both accessible</u> to the palate and psychology of young wine drinkers, and they did so without sacrificing the country's reputation to create vintages of high quality.

- ○ Australian vineyards, innovators in marketing and in product development, stormed the market with wines both accessible
- ○ Australian vineyards, innovators in marketing and in product development, stormed the market with wines that were accessible both
- ○ Australian vineyards, innovators in marketing and in product development, stormed the market with wines accessible
- ○ innovators in marketing and in product development, Australian vineyards, which stormed the market with wines accessible
- ○ innovators in marketing and in product development such as Australian vineyards stormed the market with wines accessible both

EXPLANATION

Creating a filter: In the original sentence, the word "both" is misplaced. The intended meaning is "both palate and psychology," not "both accessible and something else," so the word "both" must come after "accessible."

Applying the filter: We review the choices and find that our filter knocks out only answer choice (A). We'll have to find new points of comparison among the other choices.

Finding objective defects: we compare (B) and (C) and find them similar. In answer choice (B), could there be an objective defect in including "both"? Indeed, there is: "both... and..." is a two-part construction that must have parallel elements, but it fails to have parallel construction in (B), because "psychology" is missing the words "to the" in the remainder of the sentence, after the underlined portion. So (B) is out. In (C), meanwhile, if you discard the word "both," there is no two-part construction and the sentence is valid. So (C) looks good. Answer choice (D) actually leads to the whole thing not being a grammatical sentence with subject and predicate; "which stormed" begins one dependent clause, and "and they" later begins what is another dependent clause, since it starts with the conjunction "and," so there is no independent clause. So (D) is out. Choice (E) changes the intended meaning of the sentence by making the vineyards examples, not the point of the sentence. So (E) is out. We are down to one answer choice. The correct answer is (C).

The average height of Americans and Europeans decreased during the rapid industrialization of the 19th century, <u>a decline that is explained not so much because of a population increase as by the fact that economic inequality become more acute</u>, leading to widely disparate levels of nutrition.

- a decline that is explained not so much because of a population increase as by the fact that economic inequality become more acute
- a decline that is explained not so much by the fact that the population increased as by the fact that economic inequality become more acute
- a decline occurring not so much because of the population that was increasing as because of economic inequality having become more acute
- which occurred not so much because the population was increasing as economic inequality was also becoming more acute
- which occurred not so much because of a greater population as because economical inequality had become more acute

HEIGHT DECLINE

The average height of Americans and Europeans decreased during the rapid industrialization of the 19th century, <u>a decline that is explained not so much because of a population increase as by the fact that economic inequality become more acute</u>, leading to widely disparate levels of nutrition.

- ○ a decline that is explained not so much because of a population increase as by the fact that economic inequality become more acute
- ○ a decline that is explained not so much by the fact that the population increased as by the fact that economic inequality become more acute
- ○ a decline occurring not so much because of the population that was increasing as because of economic inequality having become more acute
- ○ which occurred not so much because the population was increasing as economic inequality was also becoming more acute
- ○ which occurred not so much because of a greater population as because economical inequality had become more acute

EXPLANATION

Creating a filter: suppose that we dislike this original sentence but can't easily find an objective error. In such a case, we can proceed to (B) and search for objective defects, noting that we have not decisively eliminated (A).

Finding objective defects: we might judge (B) less bad than (A). We'll come back to it. The verb tenses in (C) are unnecessarily involved — in "was increasing" and "having become." So (C) is out. Choice (D) has the same problems and also a parallelism error — a missing "because" after "as." Choice (E) also has a lack of parallelism between the phrase "because of," which introduces a noun, and "because," which introduces a clause. Indeed, that's also a problem with (A), between "because of" and the word "by." The correct answer is (B).

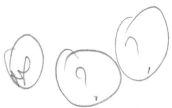

Commonly called spiral galaxies, disk <u>galaxies are formed in the universe from</u> earlier, less flat, galaxies accumulate the mass of smaller nearby galaxies and rotate faster, thus flattening.

- ○ galaxies are formed in the universe from
- ○ galaxies take form in the universe when
- ○ galaxies are formed in the universe, and when
- ○ galaxies, formed in the universe when
- ○ galaxies, formed in the universe from

DISK GALAXIES

Commonly called spiral galaxies, disk <u>galaxies are formed in the universe from</u> earlier, less flat, galaxies accumulate the mass of smaller nearby galaxies and rotate faster, thus flattening.

- ○ galaxies are formed in the universe from
- ○ galaxies take form in the universe when
- ○ galaxies are formed in the universe, and when
- ○ galaxies, formed in the universe when
- ○ galaxies, formed in the universe from

EXPLANATION

Creating a filter: In this question, the original sentence gets tied up coming out of the underlined portion. Two partial sentences have been stitched together into something that is not grammatically well-formed. "From" must lead to a noun, but the noun that follows it is meant to be the subject of the clause that follows, the clause with the verb "accumulate," and a clause cannot be as the object of a preposition. Since the "from" is the underlined part, we can must fix this problem by getting rid of the "from."

Applying the filter: our filter eliminates choices (A) and (E), since they have "from." Choice (B) looks clear and straightforward, so we can come back to it. In (C), the word "when" introduces a dependent clause that may only have a valid grammatical existence if it is followed by an independent clause, which it isn't. In other words, it starts something like, "When X, Y," but there is no clause "Y" afterward, so it's an incomplete sentence. Choice (D) turns "formed" into the beginning of a long modifying phrase, and as a result there is no proper verb or predicate corresponding to the subject "galaxies." We've eliminated all choices but one. The correct answer is (B).

The crucial difference <u>between the capabilities of a consistent market winner with those of other companies may be not in any knowledge area but</u> in the ability to develop new areas of expertise as the market evolves.

- ○ between the capabilities of a consistent market winner with those of other companies may be not in any knowledge area but
- ○ between the capabilities of a consistent market winner with those of other companies may be not in any knowledge area but instead
- ○ between the capabilities of a consistent market winner and those of other companies may be not in any knowledge area but rather
- ○ a consistent market winner's capabilities have from those of other companies may be not in any knowledge area as
- ○ of a consistent market winner's capabilities to those of other companies may not be in any knowledge area but

CONSISTENT MARKET WINNER

The crucial difference <u>between the capabilities of a consistent market winner with those of other companies may be not in any knowledge area but</u> in the ability to develop new areas of expertise as the market evolves.

○   between the capabilities of a consistent market winner with those of other companies may be not in any knowledge area but

○   between the capabilities of a consistent market winner with those of other companies may be not in any knowledge area but instead

○   between the capabilities of a consistent market winner and those of other companies may be not in any knowledge area but rather

○   a consistent market winner's capabilities have from those of other companies may be not in any knowledge area as

○   of a consistent market winner's capabilities to those of other companies may not be in any knowledge area but

EXPLANATION

Creating a filter: the original sentence is defective in its use of the word "between," which requires the word "and," not "with." So (A) is out.

Applying the filter: choice (B) is out on the same grounds as (A) — the use of "with." To narrow down the other choices, we'll have to find new defects.

Finding objective defects: choice (C) is not obviously defective, so we can come back to it. (D) and (E) take a different approach to the sentence. (D) is improper English usage; the capabilities of one market winner cannot alone "have" a difference. (E), similarly, uses "of" and "to" rather than the proper "between" and "and." The correct answer is (C).

Even though the homogeneity of the genetic record of the world's population, which is said to be consistent between individuals to one part in ten thousand, has been explained by environmental factors, it may be equally accounted for by the theory of convergent evolution.

- Even though the homogeneity of the genetic record of the world's population, which is said to be consistent between individuals to one part in ten thousand, has been explained by environmental factors, it may be equally accounted for by the theory of convergent evolution.
- Although said to be consistent between individuals to one part in ten thousand, the homogeneity of the genetic record of the world's population has been explained by environmental factors and may be equally accounted for by the theory of convergent evolution.
- Equally accounted for by the theory of convergent evolution, the homogeneity of the genetic record of the world's population, which is said to be consistent between individuals to one part in ten thousand, has been explained by environmental factors.
- Consistent between individuals to one part in ten thousand, the homogeneity of the genetic record of the world's population, even though explained by environmental factors, but is accounted for by the theory of convergent evolution.
- While the homogeneity of the genetic record of the world's population is said to be consistent between individuals to one part in ten thousand, it has been explained by environmental factors, and may be equally accounted for by the theory of convergent evolution.

GENETIC HOMOGENEITY

<u>Even though the homogeneity of the genetic record of the world's population, which is said to be consistent between individuals to one part in ten thousand, has been explained by environmental factors, it may be equally accounted for by the theory of convergent evolution.</u>

- ○ Even though the homogeneity of the genetic record of the world's population, which is said to be consistent between individuals to one part in ten thousand, has been explained by environmental factors, it may be equally accounted for by the theory of convergent evolution.
- ○ Although said to be consistent between individuals to one part in ten thousand, the homogeneity of the genetic record of the world's population has been explained by environmental factors and may be equally accounted for by the theory of convergent evolution.
- ○ Equally accounted for by the theory of convergent evolution, the homogeneity of the genetic record of the world's population, which is said to be consistent between individuals to one part in ten thousand, has been explained by environmental factors.
- ○ Consistent between individuals to one part in ten thousand, the homogeneity of the genetic record of the world's population, even though explained by environmental factors, but is accounted for by the theory of convergent evolution.
- ○ While the homogeneity of the genetic record of the world's population is said to be consistent between individuals to one part in ten thousand, it has been explained by environmental factors, and may be equally accounted for by the theory of convergent evolution.

EXPLANATION

Creating a filter: we can take our time reading the somewhat lengthy underlined sentence. Assuming we identify no error, we can move on to choice (B).

Finding objective defects: choice (B) distorts the intended meaning. The "consistent to one part in ten thousand" part is not being disputed, as (B) implies; it's just providing information about the subject the imaginary author is discussing. Choice (C) also distorts the point. The "convergent evolution" piece is the point of the sentence, but (C) sticks it at the beginning as if that point were a given. The main point of a sentence should, generally, reside in its independent clause. Choice (C) is out. Choice (D) more or less expresses the intended meaning, but it has a grammatical error; the insertion of the conjunction "but" makes it a non-sentence because it creates a clause that has a verb, "is accounted for," with no grammatical subject. Choice (D) is out. Choice (E) distorts the intended meaning in a way similar to (B). The correct answer is (A).

Producers of jazz albums tend to back artists <u>that they expect will gain popularity in the key European market, and who are</u>.

- ○ that they expect will gain popularity in the key European market, and who are
- ○ that are expected to gain popularity in the key European market, and they have
- ○ they expect to gain popularity in the key European market, and who do
- ○ being expected to gain popularity in the key European market, and have
- ○ had been expected to gain popularity in the key European market, and they have

JAZZ MARKETS

Producers of jazz albums tend to back artists <u>that they expect will gain popularity in the key European market, and who are</u>.

- ○ that they expect will gain popularity in the key European market, and who are
- ○ that are expected to gain popularity in the key European market, and they have
- ○ they expect to gain popularity in the key European market, and who do
- ○ being expected to gain popularity in the key European market, and have
- ○ had been expected to gain popularity in the key European market, and they have

EXPLANATION

Creating a filter: in the original sentence, the relative pronoun "that" should be "whom," since artists are people. That inaccuracy may not be a decisive defect, however. To improve the phrasing, I'd omit a couple words through elision without loss of clarity and say, "tend to back artists they expect to gain...," which is perfectly grammatical. We can use this prediction of the correct answer as our filter.

Applying the filter: scanning down, we can see that our prediction is quite similar to answer choice (C). Choices (B) and (E) use "they" in a new independent clause that could refer falsely to the producers, so those two are out. Choice (D) is missing a relative pronoun such as "who," and it uses a needless gerund, "being," at the beginning of the phrase. Reflecting back on (A), we can see that the future tense of "will gain popularity" lacks consistency of grammar and sense with the latter verb in "who are." The correct answer is (C).

Although they cannot always distinguish between changes limited to one part of the supply chain <u>and those that will move through it, most analysts who have watched the market typically have concluded</u> that heating-oil prices rise the year after the prices of crude oil rise.

- ○ and those that will move through it, most analysts who have watched the market typically have concluded
- ○ and the ones that will move through them, with most analysts who have watched the market typically concluding
- ○ and the ones that will move through it, most analysts who have watched it typically conclude
- ○ or those that will move through them, most analysts who have watched them typically concluded
- ○ or those that will move through them, with most analysts who have watched the market typically concluding

HEATING-OIL PRICES

Although they cannot always distinguish between changes limited to one part of the supply chain <u>and those that will move through it, most analysts who have watched the market typically have concluded</u> that heating-oil prices rise the year after the prices of crude oil rise.

- ○ and those that will move through it, most analysts who have watched the market typically have concluded
- ○ and the ones that will move through them, with most analysts who have watched the market typically concluding
- ○ and the ones that will move through it, most analysts who have watched it typically conclude
- ○ or those that will move through them, most analysts who have watched them typically concluded
- ○ or those that will move through them, with most analysts who have watched the market typically concluding

EXPLANATION

Creating a filter: in the underlined portion of the original sentence, the pronoun "those" is suspicious, because it's a pronoun. However, the pronoun refers clearly to "changes." So the original sentence may not be defective. We'll proceed to (B).

Finding objective defects: in (B), "with" is not properly a conjunction, and it's not being used to convey its actual meaning, as in "along with." So (B) is out, as is (E), which also makes the "with" mistake. Choice (C) introduces a new pronoun, "it," appearing to destroy the intended meaning of the sentence, which in that case doesn't mention the market anymore. Choice (D) has a pronoun issue: "them" should be "it," to refer to the singular "supply chain." Choice (D) is out. We are down to one. The correct answer is (A).

One of history's most popular composers, Beethoven composed throughout his entire life; his symphonies — some composed while deaf — are quite possibly performed more <u>than any</u> other composer.

- ○ than any
- ○ than any other
- ○ than are any
- ○ than those of any other
- ○ as are those of any

BEETHOVEN

One of history's most popular composers, Beethoven composed throughout his entire life; his symphonies — some composed while deaf — are quite possibly performed more <u>than any</u> other composer.

- o than any
- o than any other
- o than are any
- o than those of any other
- o as are those of any

EXPLANATION

Creating a filter: in this question, we can identify an error in the original sentence by restoring an elided portion of the sentence; an elided phrase, or elision, is a phrase which has been omitted but is clearly understood. **☐hen a sentence contains an elision, inserting the elided ☐ords ☐ill sometimes e☐pose an error, especiall☐in the use of comparisons and pronouns.** Namely, the sentence as written says, "his symphonies are performed more than any other composer *is performed*." Composers aren't performed. The intended meaning is that, "His symphonies are performed more than those of any other composer...are performed."

Applying the filter: our expectation is satisfied in choice (D). Choices (B) and (C) fail to solve the problem and still make us talk about composers when we want to talk about their symphonies. (E) is proper in making the comparison about symphonies, but "as" is incorrect. The sentence using the comparative word "more," and both "more" and "less" require always the word "than" and never "as." So (E) is out. The correct answer is (D).

<u>Investment by a scientist in an established theory, especially because it has helped to attribute unobservable causes to phenomena, makes it likely to overlook gaps in the observable data or justify them too readily.</u>

o Investment by a scientist in an established theory, especially because it has helped to attribute unobservable causes to phenomena, makes it likely to overlook gaps in the observable data or justify them too readily.

o A scientist who is invested in an established theory, especially because it has helped to attribute unobservable causes to phenomena, makes overlooking gaps in the observable data or justifying them too readily likely when they do occur.

o A scientist who is invested in an established theory is likely to overlook or justify too readily a gap in the observable data when it does appear, especially because it has helped to attribute unobservable causes to phenomena.

o Scientists' being invested in an established theory, especially because it has helped to attribute unobservable causes to phenomena, makes them likely to overlook gaps in the observable data or justifying them too readily when they do appear.

o Being invested in an established theory, especially one that has helped to attribute unobservable causes to phenomena, is likely to make scientists overlook gaps in the observable data or justify them too readily.

PERSONAL INVESTMENT

Investment by a scientist in an established theory, especially because it has helped to attribute unobservable causes to phenomena, makes it likely to overlook gaps in the observable data or justify them too readily.

○ Investment by a scientist in an established theory, especially because it has helped to attribute unobservable causes to phenomena, makes it likely to overlook gaps in the observable data or justify them too readily. *pronoun ambiguity*

○ A scientist who is invested in an established theory, especially because it has helped to attribute unobservable causes to phenomena, makes overlooking gaps in the observable data or justifying them too readily likely when they do occur.

○ A scientist who is invested in an established theory is likely to overlook or justify too readily a gap in the observable data when it does appear, especially because it has helped to attribute unobservable causes to phenomena.

○ Scientists' being invested in an established theory, especially because it has helped to attribute unobservable causes to phenomena, makes them likely to overlook gaps in the observable data or justifying them too readily when they do appear. *broken parallelism*

○ Being invested in an established theory, especially one that has helped to attribute unobservable causes to phenomena, is likely to make scientists overlook gaps in the observable data or justify them too readily.

EXPLANATION

Creating a filter: in the original sentence, the two instances of the pronoun "it" jump out as worthy of suspicion. The second "it" has no reference, and the first is ambiguous between "investment" and "theory." We can eliminate (A) on these grounds.

Applying the filter: choice (B) solves the problem in (A), but the wording in (B) indicates that the *scientist* makes gaps likely; that's contrary to the intended meaning, so (B) is out. Choice (C) has a problem with its second pronoun "it"; it's ambiguous. Choice (C) is out. Choice (D) has broken parallelism between "overlook" and "justifying." So (D) is out, and we are down to (E). Choice (E) looks good. There is no ambiguity of pronoun, and the intended meaning is clear: the investment can make scientists overlook gaps. The correct answer is (E).

The average global temperature is forecast to be 0.5 degrees Celsius higher in 50 years because this year's mean temperature is the same amount higher than that of 50 years ago.

- o The average global temperature is forecast to be 0.5 degrees Celsius higher in 50 years because this year's mean temperature is the same amount higher than that of
- o The average global temperature is forecast to rise 0.5 degrees Celsius higher in 50 years over this year because this year's mean temperature is the same amount higher than it was
- o Forecasts are for the average global temperature to be 0.5 degrees Celsius higher in 50 years than today's because today's mean temperature is the same amount higher than it was
- o It has been forecast that the average global temperature will be 0.5 degrees Celsius higher in 50 years because this year's mean temperature is the same amount higher than what it was
- o It is forecast that the average global temperature will rise 0.5 degrees Celsius higher in 50 years than this year's because this year's mean temperature is the same amount higher than it was

AVERAGE GLOBAL TEMPERATURE

The average global temperature is forecast to be 0.5 degrees Celsius higher in 50 years because this year's mean temperature is the same amount higher than that of 50 years ago.

- ○ The average global temperature is forecast to be 0.5 degrees Celsius higher in 50 years because this year's mean temperature is the same amount higher than that of
- ○ The average global temperature is forecast to rise 0.5 degrees Celsius higher in 50 years over this year because this year's mean temperature is the same amount higher than it was
- ○ Forecasts are for the average global temperature to be 0.5 degrees Celsius higher in 50 years than today's because today's mean temperature is the same amount higher than it was
- ○ It has been forecast that the average global temperature will be 0.5 degrees Celsius higher in 50 years because this year's mean temperature is the same amount higher than what it was
- ○ It is forecast that the average global temperature will rise 0.5 degrees Celsius higher in 50 years than this year's because this year's mean temperature is the same amount higher than it was

EXPLANATION

Creating a filter: the prompt is quite a mouthful. Where are the commas? We might suspect that there is a comma-related defect, but glancing over the answer choices, we can notice that there are no commas. **Sentence Correction questions rarel☐involve comma defects, ☐ith the e☐ception of comma splices, although commas are important to identif☐ modifiers and other☐ise parse sentences.** We can move on and look for objective defects.

Finding objective defects: we have a defect in (B); the pronoun "it" means the sentence discusses what "this year's mean temperature" was "50 years ago," which makes no sense and is contrary to the intended meaning. Choice (C) has the same problem. They all do! Except (A). A question that otherwise might have been quite confusing ended up crumbling under one error. The correct answer is (A).

Evidence suggests that the people who crossed the Bering Strait from Asia into North America over a land bridge were hunter-gatherers, <u>nomads living in an egalitarian society where they obtained their sustenance almost entirely from</u> wild plants and animals.

- o   nomads living in an egalitarian society where they obtained their sustenance almost entirely from
- o   nomads living in an egalitarian society that obtained its sustenance almost entirely from
- o   which means they live in an egalitarian society, obtaining their sustenance almost entirely from
- o   which means that their society is egalitarian and obtains its sustenance almost entirely from
- o   living in a society that is egalitarian and it obtains its sustenance almost entirely from

CROSSING THE BERING STRAIT

Evidence suggests that the people who crossed the Bering Strait from Asia into North America over a land bridge were hunter-gatherers, <u>nomads living in an egalitarian society where they obtained their sustenance almost entirely from</u> wild plants and animals.

- O nomads living in an egalitarian society where they obtained their sustenance almost entirely from
- O nomads living in an egalitarian society that obtained its sustenance almost entirely from
- O which means they live in an egalitarian society, obtaining their sustenance almost entirely from
- O which means that their society is egalitarian and obtains its sustenance almost entirely from
- O living in a society that is egalitarian and it obtains its sustenance almost entirely from

EXPLANATION

Creating a filter: when reading the prompt, we can pause at the word "where." A society is not a place, so "where" is incorrect. Choice (A) is out.

Applying the filter: We scan for the same error below and don't find it, so we must go back to (B) and look for new errors.

Finding objective defects: choice (B) might be correct. (C) uses "which means" incorrectly. Hunter-gatherers are included in the sentence as the people, not a term; the verb needs to be plural; if "hunter-gatherers" is to be included as a term to be defined, it needs to be in quotation marks and the preceding part of the sentence would have to be different. (C) and (D) are out. Choice (E) introduces a bogus pronoun "it," moves on to a new independent clause without a comma before "and," and uses the present tense where the past tense is required. The correct answer is (B).

where → place

The fast-flowing, narrow air currents known as jet streams, in the tropopause, where the troposphere, whose temperature decreases with altitude, gives way to the stratosphere, whose temperature increases with altitude, reach their peak strength.

- o The fast-flowing, narrow air currents known as jet streams, in the tropopause, where the troposphere, whose temperature decreases with altitude, gives way to the stratosphere, whose temperature increases with altitude,
- o In the tropopause, where the troposphere gives way to the stratosphere, decreasing and increasing with altitude, the fast-flowing, narrow air currents known as jet streams
- o In the tropopause, where the troposphere, whose temperature decreases with altitude, gives way to the stratosphere, whose temperature increases with altitude, the fast-flowing, narrow air currents known as jet streams
- o Increasing in temperature with altitude, the fast-flowing, narrow air currents known as jet streams, where the troposphere, whose temperature decreases with altitude, gives way to the stratosphere,
- o The fast-flowing, narrow air currents known as jet streams, in the tropopause, where the troposphere whose temperature decreases with altitude gives way to the stratosphere, increases in temperature with altitude and

TROPOPAUSE

The fast-flowing, narrow air currents known as jet streams, in the tropopause, where the troposphere, whose temperature decreases with altitude, gives way to the stratosphere, whose temperature increases with altitude, reach their peak strength.

○ The fast-flowing, narrow air currents known as jet streams, in the tropopause, where the troposphere, whose temperature decreases with altitude, gives way to the stratosphere, whose temperature increases with altitude,

○ In the tropopause, where the troposphere gives way to the stratosphere, decreasing and increasing with altitude, the fast-flowing, narrow air currents known as jet streams *Meaning change*

○ In the tropopause, where the troposphere, whose temperature decreases with altitude, gives way to the stratosphere, whose temperature increases with altitude, the fast-flowing, narrow air currents known as jet streams

○ Increasing in temperature with altitude, the fast-flowing, narrow air currents known as jet streams, where the troposphere, whose temperature decreases with altitude, gives way to the stratosphere, *meaning change*

○ The fast-flowing, narrow air currents known as jet streams, in the tropopause, where the troposphere whose temperature decreases with altitude gives way to the stratosphere, increases in temperature with altitude and

EXPLANATION

Creating a filter: we flow through the original sentence and may not see an error. We can move on to choice (B).

Finding objective defects: in (B), the phrase "decreasing and increasing with altitude" seems to be a distortion of the intended meaning. So (B) is probably out. (C) looks better. The subject of the main clause is near its verb, in that "troposphere" is separated by only one modifying phrase from "gives way." Also, in (C), it's easier for us to understand that all the stuff at the front of the sentence is to define the tropopause in terms of the troposphere and the stratosphere. By contrast, it's unclear in (A) what "in the tropopause" is modifying. Is it simply where jet streams reside? Therefore, (A) is out and (C) is in. Choice (D) distorts the intended meaning: "increasing temperature with altitude" is not supposed to refer to the jet streams, but rather to the stratosphere. Out. Choice (E) manages to combine the errors we just mentioned of (D) and of (A). So it's out and we are left only with (C). In this case, the answer choices were mostly jumbles of each other, and when that's the case, what's right and wrong will tend to depend on whether each sentence conveys the intended meaning correctly and clearly. The correct answer is (C).

<u>Most people's view of the sheep is an animal of less-than-average intelligence, a symbol of herd-driven foolishness; nevertheless, it ranks</u> equally with monkeys in certain cognitive tests.

o   Most people's view of the sheep is an animal of less-than-average intelligence, a symbol of herd-driven foolishness; nevertheless, it ranks
o   Most people view the sheep as an animal of less-than-average intelligence, a symbol of herd-driven foolishness, but which ranks
o   Most people view the sheep as an animal of less-than-average intelligence and as a symbol of herd-driven foolishness, but it ranks
o   Most people view the sheep to be an animal of less-than-average intelligence, a symbol of herd-driven foolishness, which ranks
o   Most people view the sheep to be a symbol of herd-driven foolishness, an animal of less-than-average intelligence, other than how it ranks,

SHEEP INTELLIGENCE

Most people's view of the sheep is an animal of less-than-average intelligence, a symbol of herd-driven foolishness; nevertheless, it ranks equally with monkeys in certain cognitive tests.

o   Most people's view of the sheep is an animal of less-than-average intelligence, a symbol of herd-driven foolishness; nevertheless, it ranks
o   Most people view the sheep as an animal of less-than-average intelligence, a symbol of herd-driven foolishness, but which ranks *meaning change (contrary needed)*
o   Most people view the sheep as an animal of less-than-average intelligence and as a symbol of herd-driven foolishness, but it ranks
o   Most people view the sheep to be an animal of less-than-average intelligence, a symbol of herd-driven foolishness, which ranks
o   Most people view the sheep to be a symbol of herd-driven foolishness, an animal of less-than-average intelligence, other than how it ranks,

EXPLANATION

Creating a filter: the grammar of the original sentence is distorting. The grammatical subject is "view," so the sentence indicates that a view is an animal, which is illogical and contrary to the intended meaning. Note that the word "animal," though a noun, is not the grammatical subject of the sentence as written, because the word "animal" is an object of the preposition "of." So (A) is out.

Applying the filter: choice (B) indicates that people view the sheep as ranking with monkeys in intelligence; that's a distortion of the intended meaning. The equality of rank, in the intended meaning, is a fact that's contrary to people's view, not in line with it. So (B) is out. Choice (D) has this same problem, so it's out. Choice (E) also has this problem, among others. Moreover, "view as" is the proper idiom, not "view to be." The correct answer is (C).

When snowfall is heavy, the snow leopard is known to descend to lower elevations and frequent mountain slopes <u>whose conditions also are favorable to</u> the leopard's prey, such as the markor.

- ○ whose conditions also are favorable to
- ○ where there are also favorable conditions to
- ○ where they also have conditions favorable to
- ○ with favorable conditions, as well, to
- ○ having conditions favorable also for

SNOW LEOPARD

When snowfall is heavy, the snow leopard is known to descend to lower elevations and frequent mountain slopes <u>whose conditions also are favorable to</u> the leopard's prey, such as the markor.

- ○ whose conditions also are favorable to
- ○ where there are also favorable conditions to
- ○ where they also have conditions favorable to
- ○ with favorable conditions, as well, to
- ○ having conditions favorable also for

EXPLANATION

Creating a filter: as we read the original sentence, we keep an eye on the placement of the word "also." But that placement could be correct, if the intended meaning is that the lower elevations, in addition to the upper elevations, have conditions favorable to the markor. We'll have to look for defects in the other choices and come back to (A).

Finding objective defects: choice (B) is defective in that "favorable" and "to" are separated by the word "conditions," violating the idiomatic usage of "favorable." Choice (B) is out. Choice (C) introduces a pronoun with no reference, "they," so it's out. Choice (D) has the same problem as (B), so it's out. Choice (E) has an idiomatic error, since "favorable for" is not proper usage. We are left with one choice. The correct answer is (A).

Dadaism, the avant-garde European artistic movement of the early twentieth century, <u>a phenomenon in which the postwar economic and moral sentiments gave birth to art that appeared to reject</u> logic and embrace chaos.

- ○ a phenomenon in which the postwar economic and moral sentiments gave birth to art that appeared to reject
- ○ a phenomenon when the postwar economic and moral sentiments were giving birth to art that appeared, rejecting
- ○ a phenomenon in which the postwar economic and moral sentiments appeared and give birth to art that rejected
- ○ was a phenomenon in which the postwar economic and moral sentiments gave birth to art that appeared to reject
- ○ was a phenomenon when the postwar economic and moral sentiments were giving birth to art appearing to reject

DADAISM

Dadaism, the avant-garde European artistic movement of the early twentieth century, <u>a phenomenon in which the postwar economic and moral sentiments gave birth to art that appeared to reject</u> logic and embrace chaos.

- ○ a phenomenon in which the postwar economic and moral sentiments gave birth to art that appeared to reject   *needs a verb*
- ○ a phenomenon when the postwar economic and moral sentiments were giving birth to art that appeared, rejecting
- ○ a phenomenon in which the postwar economic and moral sentiments appeared and give birth to art that rejected
- ○ was a phenomenon in which the postwar economic and moral sentiments gave birth to art that appeared to reject
- ○ was a phenomenon when the postwar economic and moral sentiments were giving birth to art appearing to reject

EXPLANATION

Creating a filter: the original sentence is not, in fact, a sentence. There is no verb corresponding to the grammatical subject "Dadaism." Everything from "a phenomenon" on is a modifying phrase. So (A) is out.

Applying the filter: (B) and (C) are out on the same grounds as (A), as we can see by looking at their first few words. In answer choice (E), the use of "when" is incorrect, because a "phenomenon" is not a time. The correct answer is (D).

· When → time
· Need verb in sentence

<u>Although it won't increase bank revenues to upgrade the operating systems running the nation's ATMs, it is the risks involved in failing to update the software that make that alternative more costly.</u>

- o Although it won't increase bank revenues to upgrade the operating systems running the nation's ATMs, it is the risks involved in failing to update the software that make that alternative more costly.
- o Although upgrading the operating systems running the nation's ATMs won't increase bank revenues, the risks involved in failing to update the software make that alternative more costly.
- o Even though it won't increase bank revenues if the operating systems running the nation's ATMs are upgraded, it is the risks involved in failing to update the software that could make that alternative more costly.
- o It won't increase bank revenues if and when the operating systems running the nation's ATMs are upgraded, whereas the alternative of failing to update the software is more costly, given the risks involved.
- o Upgrading the operating systems running the nation's ATMs won't increase bank revenues above today, but failing to update the software is the more costly alternative because of the risks involved.

ATM Operating Systems

Although it won't increase bank revenues to upgrade the operating systems running the nation's ATMs, it is the risks involved in failing to update the software that make that alternative more costly.

- ○ Although it won't increase bank revenues to upgrade the operating systems running the nation's ATMs, it is the risks involved in failing to update the software that make that alternative more costly.
- ○ Although upgrading the operating systems running the nation's ATMs won't increase bank revenues, the risks involved in failing to update the software make that alternative more costly.
- ○ Even though it won't increase bank revenues if the operating systems running the nation's ATMs are upgraded, it is the risks involved in failing to update the software that could make that alternative more costly.
- ○ It won't increase bank revenues if and when the operating systems running the nation's ATMs are upgraded, whereas the alternative of failing to update the software is more costly, given the risks involved.
- ○ Upgrading the operating systems running the nation's ATMs won't increase bank revenues above today, but failing to update the software is the more costly alternative because of the risks involved.

Explanation

Creating a filter: in the original sentence, we have two conversational uses of the pronoun "it" that have no actual reference. Both must go, and (A) is out. We'll seek to eliminate other answer choices with the same problem.

Applying the filter: choices (C) and (D) have the same problem as (A), so those two are out. Choice (B) has no clear defect, so we can come back to it. Choice (E) communicates the intended meaning less clearly. We've lost the meaning of where the risks come from. Risks involved in what? Therefore, (E) is inferior to (B). The correct answer is (B).

<u>Planets within the habitable zone, the shell-shaped region of space surrounding a star within which a planet could maintain liquid water on its surface, are much more likely than more distant planets to harbor atmospheres which contain water and, possibly, multicellular life.</u>

o   Planets within the habitable zone, the shell-shaped region of space surrounding a star within which a planet could maintain liquid water on its surface, are much more likely than more distant planets to harbor atmospheres which contain water and, possibly, multicellular life.

o   Planets within the habitable zone, the shell-shaped region of space surrounding a star within which a planet could maintain liquid water on its surface, which are much more likely than more distant planets to harbor atmospheres which contain water and, possibly, multicellular life.

o   Atmospheres that contain water and, possibly, multicellular life, on planets within the habitable zone, the shell-shaped region of space surrounding a star within which a planet could maintain liquid water on its surface, is the much more likely to be harbored rather than on more distant planets.

o   Atmospheres on planets within the habitable zone, the shell-shaped region of space surrounding a star within which a planet could maintain liquid water on its surface, rather than on more distant stars, are much more likely to harbor multicellular life when they contain water.

o   Rather than more distant planets, the atmospheres of planets within the habitable zone, the shell-shaped region of space surrounding a star within which a planet could maintain liquid water on its surface, are much more likely to contain water and, possibly, multicellular life.

HABITABLE ZONES

Planets within the habitable zone, the shell-shaped region of space surrounding a star within which a planet could maintain liquid water on its surface, are much more likely than more distant planets to harbor atmospheres which contain water and, possibly, multicellular life.

- ○ Planets within the habitable zone, the shell-shaped region of space surrounding a star within which a planet could maintain liquid water on its surface, are much more likely than more distant planets to harbor atmospheres which contain water and, possibly, multicellular life.
- ○ Planets within the habitable zone, the shell-shaped region of space surrounding a star within which a planet could maintain liquid water on its surface, which are much more likely than more distant planets to harbor atmospheres which contain water and, possibly, multicellular life.
- ○ Atmospheres that contain water and, possibly, multicellular life, on planets within the habitable zone, the shell-shaped region of space surrounding a star within which a planet could maintain liquid water on its surface, is the much more likely to be harbored rather than on more distant planets.
- ○ Atmospheres on planets within the habitable zone, the shell-shaped region of space surrounding a star within which a planet could maintain liquid water on its surface, rather than on more distant stars, are much more likely to harbor multicellular life when they contain water.
- ○ Rather than more distant planets, the atmospheres of planets within the habitable zone, the shell-shaped region of space surrounding a star within which a planet could maintain liquid water on its surface, are much more likely to contain water and, possibly, multicellular life.

EXPLANATION

Creating a filter: the original sentence appears to be well formed. So we can move on to (B) and see what we're able to eliminate.

Finding objective defects: choice (B) is not grammatically a sentence. The phrases starting with "the shell-shaped region" and "which are much more likely" are both modifying phrases, so the grammatical subject "planets" has no verb, and there is no independent clause. So (B) is out. In choice (C), either the verb for "atmospheres" is supposed to be "is," or "atmospheres" has no verb, but either way it fails to be a grammatical sentence. Choice (C) is out. In choice (D), the meaning is distorted. *All* stars are more likely to contain life when they retain water, but that's not really what the wording of choice (D) is saying, and it muddles the relationship between the habitable zone and the likelihood of having water. So (D) is out. Choice (E) fails early on because it grammatically compares "planets" with "atmospheres of planets." The correct answer is (A).

Invented for use in short wavelength radar during WWII, the cavity magnetron, which was able to produce electromagnetic waves at a lower frequency than had previously been possible, was the basis for the development of the common microwave oven.

- Invented for use in short wavelength radar during WWII, the cavity magnetron, which was able to produce electromagnetic waves at a lower frequency than had previously been possible,
- Invented for use in short wavelength radar during WWII, having the ability to produce electromagnetic waves at a lower frequency than had previously been possible, the cavity magnetron
- A technology invented for use in short wavelength radar during WWII, called the cavity magnetron, which was able to produce electromagnetic waves at a lower frequency than had previously been possible,
- A technology invented for use in short wavelength radar during WWII, called the cavity magnetron, which had the ability to produce electromagnetic waves at a lower frequency than had previously been possible,
- A technology invented for use in short wavelength radar during WWII and had the ability to produce electromagnetic waves at a lower frequency than had previously been possible, called the cavity magnetron,

CAVITY MAGNETRON

Invented for use in short wavelength radar during WWII, the cavity magnetron, which was able to produce electromagnetic waves at a lower frequency than had previously been possible, was the basis for the development of the common microwave oven.

- o   Invented for use in short wavelength radar during WWII, the cavity magnetron, which was able to produce electromagnetic waves at a lower frequency than had previously been possible,
- o   Invented for use in short wavelength radar during WWII, having the ability to produce electromagnetic waves at a lower frequency than had previously been possible, the cavity magnetron
- o   A technology invented for use in short wavelength radar during WWII, called the cavity magnetron, which was able to produce electromagnetic waves at a lower frequency than had previously been possible,
- o   A technology invented for use in short wavelength radar during WWII, called the cavity magnetron, which had the ability to produce electromagnetic waves at a lower frequency than had previously been possible,
- o   A technology invented for use in short wavelength radar during WWII and had the ability to produce electromagnetic waves at a lower frequency than had previously been possible, called the cavity magnetron,

EXPLANATION

Creating a filter: as we make our way through the original sentence, we may not spot any candidate for error. The phrase started with "invented" properly modifies "magnetron," for example. We'll look for objective errors and come back to (A).

Finding objective errors: in (B), putting the two long modifiers in a row is inferior style, and "having the ability" is inferior to "able," so (B) is out. Choices (C), (D) and (E) are all similar. In all three, "called the cavity magnetron" is improperly constructed as a modifier set off by commas. Properly it's an elided restrictive clause standing for "that was called the cavity magnetron" and belongs closer to "technology" and not set off by commas. Conceptually, it defines the word "technology" and should be close to it. Choices (C) through (E) also distort the intended meaning of the sentence, because the cavity magnetron is what the sentence is about and the focus has shifted away from it. The correct answer is (A).

<u>Released in 1970, the creators of MASH were two Academy Award nominees, Robert Altman, who would go on to direct The Player, and director Ingo Preminger.</u>

- O Released in 1970, the creators of MASH were two Academy Award nominees, Robert Altman, who would go on to direct The Player, and director Ingo Preminger.
- O Released in 1970, two Academy Award nominees, Robert Altman, who would go on to direct The Player, and director Ingo Preminger, created MASH.
- O Released in 1970, MASH was created by two Academy Award nominees, Robert Altman, who would go on to direct The Player, and director Ingo Preminger.
- O MASH was created by two Academy Award nominees, Robert Altman, who would go on to direct The Player, and director Ingo Preminger, and released in 1970.
- O The creators being two Academy Award nominees, Robert Altman, who would go on to direct The Player, and director Ingo Preminger, MASH was released in 1970.

M*A*S*H

Released in 1970, the creators of MASH were two Academy Award nominees, Robert Altman, who would go on to direct The Player, and director Ingo Preminger.

○ Released in 1970, the creators of MASH were two Academy Award nominees, Robert Altman, who would go on to direct The Player, and director Ingo Preminger.

○ Released in 1970, two Academy Award nominees, Robert Altman, who would go on to direct The Player, and director Ingo Preminger, created MASH.

○ Released in 1970, MASH was created by two Academy Award nominees, Robert Altman, who would go on to direct The Player, and director Ingo Preminger.

○ MASH was created by two Academy Award nominees, Robert Altman, who would go on to direct The Player, and director Ingo Preminger, and released in 1970.

○ The creators being two Academy Award nominees, Robert Altman, who would go on to direct The Player, and director Ingo Preminger, MASH was released in 1970.

EXPLANATION

Creating a filter: the original sentence has a problem early on, because grammatically it's indicating that the *creators* of MASH were released in 1970, contrary to the intended meaning.

Applying the filter: choice (B) has the same problem as (A), saying that "nominees" were released in 1970. Choice (C) fixes the problem and may be okay, so we can come back to it. In choice (D), the phrase at the end, "and released in 1970," is a would-be independent clause without a grammatical subject, and it's ambiguous. So (D) is out. Choice (E) uses the awkward participial construction "being" unnecessarily. The correct answer is (C).

The Grand Canyon, <u>which was previously thought to have been carved out by the Colorado river, was eroded away by a lava flow, according to a newer theory,</u> took on its current form at an earlier date 6 to 7 million years ago.

o which was previously thought to have been carved out by the Colorado river, was eroded away by a lava flow, according to a newer theory,

o previously thought to have been carved out by the Colorado river eroded away by a lava flow, according to a newer theory, and

o previously thought to have been carved out by the Colorado river, was eroded away by a lava flow, according to a newer theory, and

o previously thought to have been carved out by the Colorado river, according to a newer theory, it eroded away by a lava flow and

o previously thought to have been carved out by the Colorado river, according to a newer theory, which was eroded away by a lava flow and

THE GRAND CANYON

The Grand Canyon, <u>which was previously thought to have been carved out by the Colorado river, was eroded away by a lava flow, according to a newer theory,</u> took on its current form at an earlier date 6 to 7 million years ago.

- ○ which was previously thought to have been carved out by the Colorado river, was eroded away by a lava flow, according to a newer theory,
- ○ previously thought to have been carved out by the Colorado river eroded away by a lava flow, according to a newer theory, and
- ○ previously thought to have been carved out by the Colorado river, was eroded away by a lava flow, according to a newer theory, and
- ○ previously thought to have been carved out by the Colorado river, according to a newer theory, it eroded away by a lava flow and
- ○ previously thought to have been carved out by the Colorado river, according to a newer theory, which was eroded away by a lava flow and

EXPLANATION

Creating a filter: in this question, the original sentence is, in fact, not grammatically a sentence. The last phrase, starting with "took on its current form," is a predicate with no grammatical subject, since the phrase "the Grand Canyon" has already gotten a predicate earlier in the sentence in the phrase, "was eroded away by a lava flow." Therefore, answer choice (A) is out. We can look for similar issues in the predicate of the remaining options.

Applying the filter: choice (B), somewhat like (A), diverges from the intended meaning of the sentence by indicating that the Colorado River was eroded away by a lava flow. Choice (B) is out. Choice (C) is improved; the "and" makes the end of the sentence part of the same predicate as "was eroded" and we have a clear sentence. So we can come back to (C). Choice (D) is a run-on sentence / non-sentence due to the inclusion of the pronoun "it" with no conjunction. Moreover, it provides no verb for the first subject, "the Grand Canyon." Choice (D) is out. In (E), the original subject of the sentence, "the Grand Canyon," never gets a verb. The correct answer is (C).

Computer networks that run on distributed servers tend not to possess one or more single points of failure, so that, if <u>one point fails it replaces it, often by the network</u> having more than one backup server available.

- ○ one point fails it replaces it, often by the network
- ○ one point fails it is replaced, with the network often
- ○ they fail at one point they replace it, sometimes by the network
- ○ they fail at one point they are replaced, with the network often
- ○ they fail one point it is replaced, often with the network having

DISTRIBUTED NETWORKS

Computer networks that run on distributed servers tend not to possess one or more single points of failure, so that, if <u>one point fails it replaces it, often by the network</u> having more than one backup server available.

- ○ one point fails it replaces it, often by the network
- ○ one point fails it is replaced, with the network often
- ○ they fail at one point they replace it, sometimes by the network
- ○ they fail at one point they are replaced, with the network often
- ○ they fail one point it is replaced, often with the network having

EXPLANATION

Creating a filter: in the original sentence, the phrase "it replaces it" doubly raises the pronoun alert. The two "its" stand for different things ambiguously. We eliminate (A) and review the remaining answer choices for their treatment of pronouns.

Applying the filter: choice (B) uses one pronoun without ambiguity, fixing that error, but it uses "with" as a conjunction. However, we notice that we may be forced to use "with," since (D) and (E) also use "with." So we'll come back to (B). Choices (D) and (E) both have ambiguous pronouns, so they are out. Going back to (C), we see it also has pronoun errors. In choices (C) through (E), the word "they" could refer to "networks" or "points" with different meanings. So (B) is the only possible option, with or without "with." I would consider the wording of choice (B) poor English style. However, in the hierarchy of considerations, basic grammar comes first; we can use this fact to navigate the questions and worry as little as possible about style. The correct answer is (B).

<u>Because there are terms of the International Maritime Organization that stipulate that every vessel that gets an identification number also be outfitted with an automatic onboard tracking system, they have partly deterred</u> illegal fishing.

- ○ Because there are terms of the International Maritime Organization that stipulate that every vessel that gets an identification number also be outfitted with an automatic onboard tracking system, they have partly deterred
- ○ Because the terms of the International Maritime Organization stipulate that every vessel that gets an identification number also be outfitted with an automatic onboard tracking system, they partly deter
- ○ Every vessel that gets an identification number must also be outfitted with an automatic onboard tracking system by the terms of the International Maritime Organization, partly deterring
- ○ Because every vessel that gets an identification number must also be outfitted with an automatic onboard tracking system by the terms of the International Maritime Organization, this has already deterred
- ○ Because every vessel that gets an identification number must also be outfitted with an automatic onboard tracking system by the terms of the International Maritime Organization, which is already deterring

MARITIME IDs

Because there are terms of the International Maritime Organization that stipulate that every vessel that gets an identification number also be outfitted with an automatic onboard tracking system, they have partly deterred illegal fishing.

○ Because there are terms of the International Maritime Organization that stipulate that every vessel that gets an identification number also be outfitted with an automatic onboard tracking system, they have partly deterred

○ Because the terms of the International Maritime Organization stipulate that every vessel that gets an identification number also be outfitted with an automatic onboard tracking system, they partly deter

○ Every vessel that gets an identification number must also be outfitted with an automatic onboard tracking system by the terms of the International Maritime Organization, partly deterring

○ Because every vessel that gets an identification number must also be outfitted with an automatic onboard tracking system by the terms of the International Maritime Organization, this has already deterred

○ Because every vessel that gets an identification number must also be outfitted with an automatic onboard tracking system by the terms of the International Maritime Organization, which is already deterring

EXPLANATION

Creating a filter: on our way through the prompt, we snag on the pronoun "they" and must ask whether it has a clear reference. It seems to refer to the one plural word, "terms." However, at the beginning of the sentence, the phase "there are terms" uses the suspicious construction "there are." It's unnecessary and distorting, because the effect of the terms isn't due to their mere existence, but rather due to what they specifically stipulate. On those grounds, (A) is out.

Applying the filter: choice (B) removes the problem in (A) with "there are" and may be accurate, so we can come back to it. Choice (C) distorts the intended meaning, because it communicates that the *vessel* is "partly deterring." Choice (C) is out. In (D), the pronoun "this" is being used to refer to an entire clause, which is considered imprecise in English. Choice (E) uses "which" — does it have a clear reference? It could refer to "terms" sensibly, but then it would have to be plural, so (E) is out. We are left with one choice. The correct answer is (B).

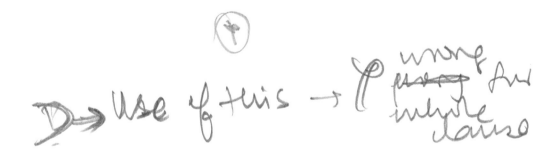

The bonobos do not form exclusive mating <u>relationships, not discriminating</u> in their sexual behavior even by sex or age.

- ○ relationships, not discriminating
- ○ relationships, and, in fact, discriminate
- ○ relationships, and they do not discriminate
- ○ relationships, so that they do not discriminate
- ○ relationships; it does not discriminate

BONOBOS' MATING

The bonobos do not form exclusive mating <u>relationships, not discriminating</u> in their sexual behavior even by sex or age.

- ○ relationships, not discriminating
- ○ relationships, and, in fact, discriminate
- ○ relationships, and they do not discriminate
- ○ relationships, so that they do not discriminate
- ○ relationships; it does not discriminate

EXPLANATION

Creating a filter: In this question, the original sentence is brief and possibly error-free, so we can move on to choice (B).

Finding objective defects: choice (B) distorts the intended meaning of the sentence. The fact that bonobos do *not* discriminate means they mate quite freely, so (B) has that part backwards. Choice (C) looks quite similar to (A); we can skip it for now. In (D), the phrase "so that" indicates that they do not form relationships *in order* not to discriminate. More properly, the first part of the statement and the second are similar, almost equivalent facts; the second one is an elaboration, not an outcome. So (D) is out. Choice (E) introduces a pronoun without reference, "it," so it's out. Deciding between (C) and (A) will really depend on the intended meaning of the sentence. Choice (C) presents the two clauses as separate, equal facts, since they are both independent clauses. Choice (A) presents them more as two aspects of the same idea, and that's truer to the meaning of the sentence. The correct answer is (A).

• Stay true to the meaning of the sentence

In some cases, two clouds may break apart from the collapsing matter that typically forms a <u>star, then holding each other in orbit</u> around their common center of mass as a binary star.

o star, then holding each other in orbit
o star, and then holding each other in orbit
o star and then hold each other in orbit
o star and then hold each other, they orbit
o star and then orbit, holding each other

Binary Star

In some cases, two clouds may break apart from the collapsing matter that typically forms a <u>star, then holding each other in orbit</u> around their common center of mass as a binary star.

- ○ star, then holding each other in orbit
- ○ star, and then holding each other in orbit
- ○ star and then hold each other in orbit
- ○ star and then hold each other, they orbit
- ○ star and then orbit, holding each other

Explanation

Creating a filter: in the original sentence, there's a problem with the conjunction. If one thing happens *and* then another thing happens, it's clearest to use the word "and." The participial phrase starting with "holding" would be more appropriate if the events were largely simultaneous and largely related. And "then" is not a conjunction.

Applying the filter: choices (B) and (E) have the same problem as (A) does. Choice (C) correctly and simply expresses the fact that one event comes after the other, using two verbs in a compound predicate. Choice (D) is not a sentence, since "they orbit" initiates a new independent clause without a conjunction. The correct answer is (C).

then → not a conjunction

<u>A nuclear test explosion was detonated recently in the Pacific Ocean, creating a substantial blast with a yield of 7.3 kilotons, or magnitude 5.1 on the Richter scale if it had been measured as an earthquake.</u>

○ A nuclear test explosion was detonated recently in the Pacific Ocean, creating a substantial blast with a yield of 7.3 kilotons, or magnitude 5.1 on the Richter scale if it had been measured as an earthquake.

○ A nuclear test explosion detonated recently in the Pacific Ocean created a substantial blast with a yield of 7.3 kilotons, or magnitude 5.1 on the Richter scale as an earthquake.

○ When a nuclear test explosion was detonated recently in the Pacific Ocean, it created a substantial blast with a yield of 7.3 kilotons; qualifying it to be magnitude 5.1 on the Richter scale if an earthquake.

○ A nuclear test explosion detonated recently in the Pacific Ocean created a substantial blast with a yield of 7.3 kilotons; an earthquake with that force would measure as magnitude 5.1 on the Richter scale.

○ When a nuclear test explosion was detonated recently in the Pacific Ocean, its substantial blast, which would be deemed magnitude 5.1 on the Richter scale for an earthquake, yielded 7.3 kilotons.

TEST EXPLOSION

A nuclear test explosion was detonated recently in the Pacific Ocean, creating a substantial blast with a yield of 7.3 kilotons, or magnitude 5.1 on the Richter scale if it had been measured as an earthquake.

- ○ A nuclear test explosion was detonated recently in the Pacific Ocean, creating a substantial blast with a yield of 7.3 kilotons, or magnitude 5.1 on the Richter scale if it had been measured as an earthquake.
- ○ A nuclear test explosion detonated recently in the Pacific Ocean created a substantial blast with a yield of 7.3 kilotons, or magnitude 5.1 on the Richter scale as an earthquake.
- ○ When a nuclear test explosion was detonated recently in the Pacific Ocean, it created a substantial blast with a yield of 7.3 kilotons; qualifying it to be magnitude 5.1 on the Richter scale if an earthquake.
- ○ A nuclear test explosion detonated recently in the Pacific Ocean created a substantial blast with a yield of 7.3 kilotons; an earthquake with that force would measure as magnitude 5.1 on the Richter scale.
- ○ When a nuclear test explosion was detonated recently in the Pacific Ocean, its substantial blast, which would be deemed magnitude 5.1 on the Richter scale for an earthquake, yielded 7.3 kilotons.

EXPLANATION

Creating a filter: as we blast our way through the original sentence, we should pause at the ambiguous pronoun "it." Furthermore, properly we should not use the word "if," because there is not really a condition in the intended meaning of the sentence. We'll look for another answer choice with a more precise expression.

Applying the filter: choice (B) does not improve on the "if" because the phrase "as an earthquake" seems to state that the blast *is* or *could be* an earthquake, so we have a distortion of the intended meaning. In (C), the semicolon is used improperly, leaving a sentence fragment on the latter side. Choice (D) uses the semicolon properly and avoids the problems of (A) and (B), though it's longer. In Choice (E), we lose the whole point that 5.1 on one scale is 7.3 on another. The correct answer is (D).

Panama seceded from Colombia in 1903, <u>except for Panama constructing a canal</u>, the two countries continued on similar courses for the next decade.

- ○ except for Panama constructing a canal
- ○ except in constructing Panama's canal
- ○ but other than in Panama's construction of a canal
- ○ but other than the construction of a canal in Panama
- ○ but other than in constructing the Panama canal

PANAMA AND COLOMBIA

Panama seceded from Colombia in 1903, <u>except for Panama constructing a canal</u>, the two countries continued on similar courses for the next decade.

○   except for Panama constructing a canal
○   except in constructing Panama's canal
○   but other than in Panama's construction of a canal
○   but other than the construction of a canal in Panama
○   but other than in constructing the Panama canal

EXPLANATION

Creating a filter: as we cut our way through the original sentence, we can see that it's not actually grammatically a sentence. There are two independent clauses without a conjunction joining them. We'll look for this error in the other answer choices.

Applying the filter: choice (B) has the same problem. Choice (D) sets up an illogical comparison between "construction" in the answer choice and "countries" after the answer choice. Choices (C) and (E) are similar to each other. Their main difference is in the meaning conveyed; (C) conveys that Panama constructed the canal without Colombia, and (E) conveys that the two countries constructed it together. The sentence says that these two countries *otherwise* continued on similar courses, as indicated by the words "but other than." That means they didn't continue on similar courses with respect to the canal. Choice (E), therefore, doesn't fit the logic of the sentence. The correct answer is (C).

In August, 2013, India was the first nation on record to declare dolphins <u>to be non-human persons with their own rights and ban the capture and import of them</u> for the purpose of commercial entertainment.

- ○ to be non-human persons with their own rights and ban the capture and import of them
- ○ should be non-human persons with their own rights and ban the capture and import of them
- ○ as being non-human persons with their own rights and banning the capture and import of them
- ○ as if non-human persons with their own rights and ban the capture and import of them
- ○ non-human persons with their own rights and to ban the capture and import of them

NON-HUMAN PERSONS

In August, 2013, India was the first nation on record to declare dolphins <u>to be non-human persons with their own rights and ban the capture and import of them</u> for the purpose of commercial entertainment.

- ○ to be non-human persons with their own rights and ban the capture and import of them
- ○ should be non-human persons with their own rights and ban the capture and import of them
- ○ as being non-human persons with their own rights and banning the capture and import of them
- ○ as if non-human persons with their own rights and ban the capture and import of them
- ○ non-human persons with their own rights and to ban the capture and import of them

EXPLANATION

Creating a filter: supposing that we don't find an error in the original sentence, we can set out to eliminate the other answer choices and come back to (A).

Finding objective defects: choice (B) is wrong in the use of "should be." That would be putting a moral burden on the dolphins for their state of existence. Or, it would mean that dolphins should be something they are not, quite contrary to the intended meaning, which is to say what dolphins *are*. Choice (B) is out. Choice (C) is out for the unnecessary use of "being." In choice (D), the phrase "as if" conveys a comparison with something that is contrary to fact, and in the intended meaning, there is not actually a comparison or a contrary-to-fact element. Choice (E) looks good, so we are left with (E) and (A). Choice (A) has "to be" at the beginning, and (E) uses the infinitive "to ban." (E) is better on both counts. The nation declared dolphins non-human persons; the words "to be" are superfluous. The correct answer is (E).

Today, because of the greater efficiency of communicating online, the number of people who can participate in a given meeting is <u>double the number that it has been</u> in 1995.

- ○ double the number that it has been
- ○ twice as many as it was
- ○ as much as twice the number it was
- ○ two times as many people as there were
- ○ a doubling of the people as

MEETING SIZE

Today, because of the greater efficiency of communicating online, the number of people who can participate in a given meeting is <u>double the number that it has been</u> in 1995.

- ○ double the number that it has been
- ○ twice as many as it was
- ○ as much as twice the number it was
- ○ two times as many people as there were
- ○ a doubling of the people as

EXPLANATION

Creating a filter: in this question, the original sentence uses the present perfect where simple past tense is in order, because 1995 is over, as the sentence implies, and because the happenings of 1995 are not a current development. So (A) is out. We can eliminate answer choices by examining either the verb tense or the way the comparison is constructed.

Applying the filter: choice (B) might be good; it uses "as" with another "as" correctly. In (C), "as much as" is used colloquially, not precisely; it should be used to convey equivalence and for that purpose here, it's needlessly wordy. In (D), the phrase "there were" changes the meaning of the sentence; now it's talking about how many people existed, not how many people could participate in a given meeting. It's also not parallel; it should compare the number of people who *can* with the number of people who *could*. In (E), "doubling" is a gerund, the kind of word we use to form a noun only when a simple noun doesn't exist — or, in this case, the adjective "twice." The correct answer is (B).

Gene therapy, the use of DNA as a drug to treat disease, has potential applications such as "gene doping," <u>treating single gene defects</u> in individuals, and the elimination of certain malicious genes from the DNA passed on to patient's offspring.

- ○ treating single gene defects
- ○ the treatment of single gene defects
- ○ treat single gene defects
- ○ to treat single gene defects
- ○ single gene defects that can be treated

GENE THERAPY

Gene therapy, the use of DNA as a drug to treat disease, has potential applications such as "gene doping," <u>treating single gene defects</u> in individuals, and the elimination of certain malicious genes from the DNA passed on to patient's offspring.

- o   treating single gene defects
- o   the treatment of single gene defects
- o   treat single gene defects
- o   to treat single gene defects
- o   single gene defects that can be treated

EXPLANATION

Creating a filter: the original sentence has a defect. To match the rest of the sentence, the phrase "treating single gene defects" should be in the form of a noun. A noun, in its place, will be unambiguous in describing what gene doping is. As written, the phrase potentially describes what gene doping is doing, as if Mr. Gene Doping were leaning over a table, treating single gene defects. So we eliminate (A) and can filter the answer choices by looking for a noun phrase to replace "treating single gene defects."

Applying the filter: our filter points us to choices (B) and (E). Choice (E), however, expresses something other than the intended meaning; it says that gene doping *is* the single gene defects. So (E) is out. (C) is not grammatical; it includes a verb that has no subject. The infinitive in (D) is meant to convey purpose or intention, but the function of the phrase is as an appositive that modifies gene doping, and such an appositive is simply an equal sign, grammatically speaking. Gene doping equals the treatment of single gene defects. The correct answer is (B).

A data software company founded this year claims <u>given access to a client company's database that it can provide</u> various types of analysis of unstructured data within various specified levels of security controls.

- ○ given access to a client company's database that it can provide
- ○ given access to a client company's database it has the ability of providing
- ○ the capability, given access to a client company's database, of providing
- ○ to be able, given access to a client company's database, to provide
- ○ being capable of providing, given access to a client company's database,

CLIENT DATABASE

A data software company founded this year claims <u>given access to a client company's database that it can provide</u> various types of analysis of unstructured data within various specified levels of security controls.

- ○ given access to a client company's database that it can provide
- ○ given access to a client company's database it has the ability of providing
- ○ the capability, given access to a client company's database, of providing
- ○ to be able, given access to a client company's database, to provide
- ○ being capable of providing, given access to a client company's database,

EXPLANATION

Creating a filter: the original sentence has a defect. Namely, the company is making a claim, and the claim is introduced by the word "that," but the detail about getting access to the database is part of the claim, so it should be inside the clause starting with "that." So (A) is out. We can filter for answer choices that properly express the claim of the company.

Applying the filter: the other answer choices differ in how they start. After "claims," there are a few valid possibilities. First, we can get the word "that," with a statement inside it representing the claim. Second, the word "that" can be elided, and we still can get the claim as a complete sentence; in such a case, the first word might be "it," as in, "the company claims it can provide all sorts of analysis." There is another valid possibility, which is represented by (D): to compact the content of the claim into an infinitive. (D) is correct. Additional objective defects in the other answers are the following. In (B), "ability of providing" is not proper idiom. In (C), "capability of providing" is similarly wrong, and the meaning is distorted in saying the company "claims this capability"; it sounds like they are seizing an object. And (E) uses the gerund "being" unnecessarily. The correct answer is (D).

Eugene Fama's theory <u>of there being "efficient" financial markets, meaning that an investor, given widely available information, cannot consistently achieve returns in excess of average market returns, is still respected</u>.

- ○ of there being "efficient" financial markets, meaning that an investor, given widely available information, cannot consistently achieve returns in excess of average market returns, is still respected
- ○ of "efficient" financial markets whose average returns cannot be exceeded by an investor, given widely available information, is still respected
- ○ that financial markets are "efficient," and therefore an investor given widely available information cannot consistently achieve returns in excess of average market returns, is still respected
- ○ which is that there can be no investor given widely available information who consistently achieves returns in excess of average returns in an "efficient" financial market is still respected
- ○ which is still respected is that financial markets are "efficient," in that an investor given widely available information cannot consistently achieve returns in excess of average market returns

EFFICIENT MARKETS

Eugene Fama's theory <u>of there being "efficient" financial markets, meaning that an investor, given widely available information, cannot consistently achieve returns in excess of average market returns, is still respected</u>.

- o of there being "efficient" financial markets, meaning that an investor, given widely available information, cannot consistently achieve returns in excess of average market returns, is still respected
- o of "efficient" financial markets whose average returns cannot be exceeded by an investor, given widely available information, is still respected
- o that financial markets are "efficient," and therefore an investor given widely available information cannot consistently achieve returns in excess of average market returns, is still respected
- o which is that there can be no investor given widely available information who consistently achieves returns in excess of average returns in an "efficient" financial market is still respected
- o which is still respected is that financial markets are "efficient," in that an investor given widely available information cannot consistently achieve returns in excess of average market returns

EXPLANATION

Creating a filter: we can stop early in the original sentence, because we come across the words "there being," an unnecessary gerund. It can simply be dropped; we are talking about Fama's "theory of efficient financial markets." Let's eliminate (A) and move on to the answer choices.

Applying the filter: Choice (B) distorts the intended meaning, because it doesn't make clear that having average returns that can't be exceeded is the *definition* of what makes a market efficient; with the word "whose," that fact is coming across as additional information about the markets. And the modifier "given widely available information" is floating in space, rather than as a condition for not exceeding the average returns. So (B) is out. Choice (C) is better, so we can come back to (C). In choice (D), the use of "which" would initiative a nonrestrictive clause; in other words, it implies that the theory is uniquely defined, in which case the "which" phrase must be set off by commas. It seems to indicate that Fama has only one theory. The phrase "there can be no investor" also expresses the idea inaccurately, because Fama is really talking about what existing investors are able to do, not what kinds of investors are allowed to exist by the rules of physics or something. Choice (D) is out. Choice (E) has another "which" clause that needs commas, and (E) also distorts the meaning by taking the main point — the fact that the theory is still respected — and presenting it as a minor fact about the theory. And it presents the definition as the main point. So (E) is out. The correct answer is (C).

He succeeded more as a public novelty compared to a presidential candidate, Ross Perot nevertheless established in the 1992 and 1996 campaigns that candidates running outside the two major U.S. parties could have an impact on the national discourse.

- ○ He succeeded more as a public novelty compared to a presidential candidate
- ○ Being more successful as a public novelty as compared to a presidential candidate
- ○ Successful more as a public novelty than as a presidential candidate
- ○ Although he was more successful as a public novelty when compared to a public candidate
- ○ He had been more successful as a public novelty than a presidential candidate

ROSS PEROT

<u>He succeeded more as a public novelty compared to a presidential candidate</u>, Ross Perot nevertheless established in the 1992 and 1996 campaigns that candidates running outside the two major U.S. parties could have an impact on the national discourse.

- ○ He succeeded more as a public novelty compared to a presidential candidate
- ○ Being more successful as a public novelty as compared to a presidential candidate
- ○ Successful more as a public novelty than as a presidential candidate
- ○ Although he was more successful as a public novelty when compared to a public candidate
- ○ He had been more successful as a public novelty than a presidential candidate

EXPLANATION

Creating a filter: the original sentence includes two independent clauses without a conjunction, which would go between "candidate" and "Ross," so the sentence is a run-on. Choice (A) is out. We can start with the other answer choices by evaluating subject and verb.

Applying the filter: choice (B) fixes the error in (A) but uses the awkward word "being" unnecessarily. Choice (C) sounds good. Choice (D) has a defect in the phrase "when compared to." The intended meaning does not involve time, so "when" is incorrect, and the comparative "more" should be paired simply with the word "than," as in (C). Choice (E), like (A), is an independent clause that creates a run-on. The correct answer is (C).

Known as the Tasmanian Tiger, the thylacine, <u>a species most observers agree to be made extinct by hunting by humans,</u> was the largest known carnivorous marsupial of modern times.

○   a species most observers agree to be made extinct by hunting by humans,
○   a species most observers agree that has been made extinct by human hunting,
○   a species that most observers agree has been made extinct by humans' hunting,
○   which most observers agree on as a species made extinct by humans' hunting
○   which most observers agree to be a species made extinct by humans hunting

Tasmanian Tiger

Known as the Tasmanian Tiger, the thylacine, <u>a species most observers agree to be made extinct by hunting by humans,</u> was the largest known carnivorous marsupial of modern times.

- ○ a species most observers agree to be made extinct by hunting by humans,
- ○ a species most observers agree that has been made extinct by human hunting,
- ○ a species that most observers agree has been made extinct by humans' hunting,
- ○ which most observers agree on as a species made extinct by humans' hunting
- ○ which most observers agree to be a species made extinct by humans hunting

Explanation

Creating a filter: the original sentence has problems near the phrase "be made extinct." As written, the sentence fails to convey the intended meaning. The meaning as written might indicate that the species is made extinct on a regular basis, whereas, in fact, it's something that has happened and completed. The meaning could be expressed properly as, "a species most observers agree to have been made extinct." So (A) is out. We'll look for a simple past tense instead of the infinite "to be."

Applying the filter: choice (B) has a defect: "that" is misplaced in coming after "most observers agree." If we use the word "that," we introduce a clause, and there is no verb for this clause. So (B) is out. Choice (C) uses "that" in a in a valid clause. The words "humans' hunting" is a little awkward, but it's grammatically correct. We can come back to (C). Choices (D) and (E) both have problems. In (D), the observers are not quite agreeing on the right thing. The intended meaning is that they agree on the fact and method of extinction, not the identification of species. Choice (E) also has that problem. In (D), the word "as" is not proper usage to equate "species" logically whether the thylacine. In (E), the infinitive "to be" has the same problems identified in (A). So (D) and (E) are out. The correct answer is (C).

The use of the battery-powered devices known as e-cigarettes may have the potential to lessen smoking rates, but <u>until it has been demonstrated not to have adverse side effects or increase addiction, especially in children, it will not be recommended</u>.

o   until it has been demonstrated not to have adverse side effects or increase addiction, especially in children, it will not be recommended
o   it will not be recommended before it has been demonstrated, especially in children, not to have adverse side effects or increase addiction
o   demonstrating that it does not have adverse side effects or increase addiction, especially in children, it can be recommended
o   without adverse side effects or increased addiction, especially in children, demonstrated, it will not be recommended
o   without a demonstrated lack of side effects or increased addiction, especially in children, it would not be recommended

E-CIGARETTES

The use of the battery-powered devices known as e-cigarettes may have the potential to lessen smoking rates, but <u>until it has been demonstrated not to have adverse side effects or increase addiction, especially in children, it will not be recommended</u>.

○ until it has been demonstrated not to have adverse side effects or increase addiction, especially in children, it will not be recommended

○ it will not be recommended before it has been demonstrated, especially in children, not to have adverse side effects or increase addiction

○ demonstrating that it does not have adverse side effects or increase addiction, especially in children, it can be recommended

○ without adverse side effects or increased addiction, especially in children, demonstrated, it will not be recommended

○ without a demonstrated lack of side effects or increased addiction, especially in children, it would not be recommended

EXPLANATION

Creating a filter: as we engage the prompt, we zero in on the pronouns. Pronoun errors, as we have discussed, are common and relatively easy to spot. However, both instances of "it" in this sentence can uniformly and sensibly refer to "use." We can skip (A) and come back to it.

Finding objective defects: the word order is awkward in (B) and the use of "before" imprecise. Moreover, the modifier "especially in children" is misplaced: in the intended meaning, we don't care where and how the demonstrating happens; we care that the bad stuff is absent especially in children. So (B) is out. Choices (C) and (D) and (E) all have a distortion of meaning, because they all are ambiguous as to whether or not the demonstrating has already happened. For example, (D) seems to express that the use *doesn't* have side effects but *won't* be recommended. So those three are out. The correct answer is (A).

Sigmund Freud, considered by some the father of modern psychology, developed his theory of psychoanalysis by establishing a conception of the human subconscious and <u>he applied that idea to the interpretation of dreams</u>.

- ○ he applied that idea to the interpretation of dreams
- ○ applied that idea in the interpretation of dreams
- ○ applied it to the interpretation of dreams
- ○ applying that idea to the interpretation of dreams
- ○ applying that the idea is the interpretation of dreams

THEORY OF PSYCHOANALYSIS

Sigmund Freud, considered by some the father of modern psychology, developed his theory of psychoanalysis by establishing a conception of the human subconscious and <u>he applied that idea to the interpretation of dreams</u>.

- ○ he applied that idea to the interpretation of dreams
- ○ applied that idea in the interpretation of dreams
- ○ applied it to the interpretation of dreams
- ○ applying that idea to the interpretation of dreams
- ○ applying that the idea is the interpretation of dreams

EXPLANATION

Creating a filter: the original sentence is defective. There should be a comma before the words "and he applied," since there are two independent clauses. There is also a problem of meaning; the fact that there are two independent clauses conveys the two items as mostly independent facts, which they are not; applying the idea was part of what Freud did to develop his theory, not a separate act. So (A) is out.

Applying the filter: choices (B) and (C) create the same distortion of meaning as (A). Choice (D) fixes the problem. Choice (E) is nonsensical and so it's out. The correct answer is (D).

According to one source, 11 percent of the population in France earns less annual income than the poverty line, <u>while in Germany it is just 8 percent</u>.

- ○ while in Germany it is just 8 percent
- ○ compared to Germany, where just 8 percent does
- ○ whereas just 8 percent of the population in Germany does
- ○ whereas just over 8 percent of the income less than the line is in Germany
- ○ compared with the income less than the poverty line in Germany, where it is just 8 percent

POVERTY LINES

According to one source, 11 percent of the population in France earns less annual income than the poverty line, <u>while in Germany it is just 8 percent</u>.

- ○ while in Germany it is just 8 percent
- ○ compared to Germany, where just 8 percent does
- ○ whereas just 8 percent of the population in Germany does
- ○ whereas just over 8 percent of the income less than the line is in Germany
- ○ compared with the income less than the poverty line in Germany, where it is just 8 percent

EXPLANATION

Creating a filter: the original sentence features a comparison and a pronoun. We can start with the pronoun "it," which does not have a proper reference. Grammatically, "it" could stand for 11 percent of the population in France, annual income, or the poverty line, so it's ambiguous — and none of the options make sense. Choice (A) is out. We'll look for a solution to the pronoun issue, while evaluating the comparison.

Applying the filter: choice (B) has a bad comparison; nothing preceding the comma — for example, 11 percent — is logically comparable to "Germany." Choice (C) might be right. Choice (D) conveys a strange meaning; it's not talking about the percentage in Germany in poverty, but rather the percentage of the poor in Germany. Choice (E) is a mishmash of previously identified problems. The correct answer is (C).

The term "negative feedback" comes originally not from psychology, but from electronics, which uses the term to describe a part of a circuit that detects a positive signal and <u>which, in response, takes action to diminish that signal</u>.

- which, in response, takes action to diminish that signal
- which take action to diminish that signal, in response
- by taking action, in response, to diminish that signal
- is to take action, in response, to diminish that signal
- who takes action diminishing that signal in turn

NEGATIVE FEEDBACK

The term "negative feedback" comes originally not from psychology, but from electronics, which uses the term to describe a part of a circuit that detects a positive signal and <u>which, in response, takes action to diminish that signal</u>.

- which, in response, takes action to diminish that signal
- which take action to diminish that signal, in response
- by taking action, in response, to diminish that signal
- is to take action, in response, to diminish that signal
- who takes action diminishing that signal in turn

EXPLANATION

Creating a filter: in this question, the underlined phrase appears to be defect-free. The phrase starting with "which" refers to "part," as an additional description of the part of the circuit that has been defined by "that detects a positive signal." Choice (A) may be correct, so we'll look for defects in the other choices and come back to it.

Finding objective defects: choice (B) incorrectly uses the grammatically plural verb "take" to refer to the grammatically singular "part." Choice (C) distorts the meaning: it indicates, nonsensically, that this special part of the circuit achieves its detection of the positive signal by diminishing it. Choice (C) is out. In (D), using the infinite with the verb "to be" in this way conveys a semi-moral sense of obligation that is appropriate only for humans and other moral actors. So (D) is out. And speaking of people, (E) uses the relative pronoun "who" as if the circuit were a person. The correct answer is (A).

Behavioral psychology studies have yielded evidence <u>that indicates that people tend to seek out evidence that will confirm their hypotheses, and failing to ask</u> disconfirming questions.

- o that indicates that people tend to seek out evidence that will confirm their hypotheses, and failing to ask
- o that has indicated people tend to seek out evidence that will confirm their hypotheses, failing to ask
- o indicating that that people tend to seek out evidence that will confirm their hypotheses with a failure to ask
- o to indicate that people tended to seek out evidence that will confirm their hypotheses and failed to ask
- o indicating that people tend to seek out evidence that will confirm their hypotheses and fail to ask

CONFIRMING EVIDENCE

Behavioral psychology studies have yielded evidence <u>that indicates that people tend to seek out evidence that will confirm their hypotheses, and failing to ask</u> disconfirming questions.

- ○ that indicates that people tend to seek out evidence that will confirm their hypotheses, and failing to ask
- ○ that has indicated people tend to seek out evidence that will confirm their hypotheses, failing to ask
- ○ indicating that that people tend to seek out evidence that will confirm their hypotheses with a failure to ask
- ○ to indicate that people tended to seek out evidence that will confirm their hypotheses and failed to ask
- ○ indicating that people tend to seek out evidence that will confirm their hypotheses and fail to ask

EXPLANATION

Creating a filter: the original sentence fails to be a grammatical sentence, thanks to the word "and." The phrase after the comma is not part of a list, not a modifier, not the predicate to any sentence, and not an independent clause. Choice (A) is out. We'll look for a choice that solves the basic subject-verb issue.

Applying the filter: choice (B) solves the problem in (A), though it switches the tense of "indicates" to "has indicated." The indicating is a generality, so it should be expressed in the present tense, and choice (B) is eliminated. Choice (C) leaves ambiguous what the "failure to ask" is "with." It seems to say, for example, that people are thinking about hypotheses and the failure together and confirming them both. So (C) is out. Choice (D) has past tenses that are out of place, again, in expressing this finding, which is a generality. We're left with choice (E), which is defect-free. The correct answer is (E).

Although a cause for concern in farmers, inflammation in female dairy cattle, which occurs commonly after they give birth — many disorders, including metabolic diseases such as ketosis and fatty liver, are known to occur at this time — it is believed to play a beneficial role in the complex process of going from late pregnancy to lactation.

- o Although a cause for concern among farmers, inflammation in female dairy cattle, which occurs commonly after they give birth
- o Although inflammation in female dairy cattle, which occurs commonly after they give birth, is a cause for concern among farmers
- o Although a cause for concern among farmers, inflammation in female dairy cattle, occurring commonly after they give birth
- o Occurring commonly after they give birth, inflammation in female dairy cattle is a cause for concern among farmers
- o Inflammation in female dairy cattle, which occurs commonly after they give birth, although it is a cause for concern among farmers

Dairy Cattle

<u>Although a cause for concern in farmers, inflammation in female dairy cattle, which occurs commonly after they give birth</u> — many disorders, including metabolic diseases such as ketosis and fatty liver, are known to occur at this time — it is believed to play a beneficial role in the complex process of going from late pregnancy to lactation.

o   Although a cause for concern among farmers, inflammation in female dairy cattle, which occurs commonly after they give birth
o   Although inflammation in female dairy cattle, which occurs commonly after they give birth, is a cause for concern among farmers
o   Although a cause for concern among farmers, inflammation in female dairy cattle, occurring commonly after they give birth
o   Occurring commonly after they give birth, inflammation in female dairy cattle is a cause for concern among farmers
o   Inflammation in female dairy cattle, which occurs commonly after they give birth, although it is a cause for concern among farmers

Explanation

Creating a filter: the original sentence is defective. Namely, the portion before the dash gives us the subject of a sentence, "inflammation," and that subject never receives a grammatical predicate after the dash, because a new grammatical subject is introduced with "it." So (A) is out. We need a complete clause with subject and verb prior to the dash, not a hanging grammatical subject.

Applying the filter: (C) and (E) are both hanging subjects, so we're down to (B) and (D).

Finding objective defects: plugging (B) into the original sentence sounds good. Plugging in (D) sounds wrong. The reason is that, since there is no conjunction after the dashes and the clause after the dashes is an independent clause, the clause before the dashes must be dependent. The word "although" does the trick to make (B) dependent. The correct answer is (B).

Download the free SC Strategy Sheets at GMATFree.com/SC-Strategy-Sheets

The term "sustainable" is widely applied to any practice that minimizes environmental impact, but in the case of building material <u>it is a substance that is</u> recycled or contains lower volumes of volatile organic compounds.

- ○ it is a substance that is
- ○ it is a substance
- ○ they are substances that are
- ○ it designates a substance that is
- ○ it is in reference to a substance

SUSTAINABLE MATERIAL

The term "sustainable" is widely applied to any practice that minimizes environmental impact, but in the case of building material <u>it is a substance that is</u> recycled or contains lower volumes of volatile organic compounds.

- ○   it is a substance that is
- ○   it is a substance
- ○   they are substances that are
- ○   it designates a substance that is
- ○   it is in reference to a substance

EXPLANATION

   Creating a filter: when we read the original sentence, we should examine the pronoun "it." The reference is clear: "it" refers to the first three words of the sentence, "the term 'sustainable.'" But that means the sentence isn't saying what it's trying to say. It's saying, "The term 'sustainable' is a substance" that does some things. But the term "sustainable" isn't a substance; it's a term, a word. We need something more like, "The term 'sustainable' means a substance," or, better, it refers to a substance that is recycled. We'll look for that.

   Applying the filter: Looking for that in the answer choices, we find (D), which uses a different verb but is otherwise exactly what we were looking for. Choice (E) is a little awkward and is missing the words "that is," distorting the meaning of the end of the sentence. The correct answer is (D).

In the *Surgeon General's Report: The Health Consequences of Smoking: 50 Years of Progress,* researchers claim that new regulations <u>requiring that any movie depicting smoking receives an adult rating drives</u> rates down further.

- ○ requiring that any movie depicting smoking receives an adult rating drives
- ○ requiring that any movie depicting smoking receive an adult rating would drive
- ○ that require any movie depicting smoking to receive an adult rating is driving
- ○ to require any movie depicting smoking to receive an adult rating drives
- ○ to require any movie depicting smoking to receive an adult rating to drive

SMOKING RATES

In the *Surgeon General's Report: The Health Consequences of Smoking: 50 Years of Progress,* researchers claim that new regulations <u>requiring that any movie depicting smoking receives an adult rating drives</u> rates down further.

- ○ requiring that any movie depicting smoking receives an adult rating drives
- ○ requiring that any movie depicting smoking receive an adult rating would drive
- ○ that require any movie depicting smoking to receive an adult rating is driving
- ○ to require any movie depicting smoking to receive an adult rating drives
- ○ to require any movie depicting smoking to receive an adult rating to drive

EXPLANATION

Creating a filter: our ear may detect something wrong in the original sentence. The verb "receives" should be in the subjunctive mood, as "receive," since it is within a clause of something that is being "required." Choice (A) is out. We'll look for the subjunctive mood.

Applying the filter: choice (B) has the subjunctive correct. It introduces the conditional tense in "would drive," but, come to think of it, that makes sense; the researchers are predicting the result of a hypothetical action. So (B) may be correct. Choice (C) has a mismatch between grammatically plural "regulations" and grammatically singular "is driving," so it's eliminated. Choice (D) has the same problem. Choice (E) distorts the meaning; driving rates down further now sounds like part of the requirement. The correct answer is (B).

claim → subjunctive
would → conditional
(hypothetical)

 Download the free SC Strategy Sheets at GMATFree.com/SC-Strategy-Sheets

The brightness on Earth of such celestial bodies <u>like stars invariably depends both on the radius of the luminescent object and its temperature</u>.

- ○ like stars invariably depends both on the radius of the luminescent object and its temperature
- ○ like stars invariably depends both on the radius of the luminescent object and on its temperature
- ○ as stars invariably depends on both the radius of the luminescent object and on its temperature
- ○ as stars invariably depends both on the radius of the luminescent object and its temperature
- ○ as stars invariably depends both on the radius of the luminescent object and on its temperature

CELESTIAL BRIGHTNESS

The brightness on Earth of such celestial bodies <u>like stars invariably depends both on the radius of the luminescent object and its temperature</u>.

- ○ like stars invariably depends both on the radius of the luminescent object and its temperature
- ○ like stars invariably depends both on the radius of the luminescent object and on its temperature
- ○ as stars invariably depends on both the radius of the luminescent object and on its temperature
- ○ as stars invariably depends both on the radius of the luminescent object and its temperature
- ○ as stars invariably depends both on the radius of the luminescent object and on its temperature

EXPLANATION

Creating a filter: the words "such" and "like" do not operate together as they have been combined in the original sentence. The proper idiom is "such as." So (A) is out and we'll for a solution such as the phrase "such as."

Applying the filter: we are left with choices (C) through (E). Within those choices, there is variation in the placement of "both." It can be "both on X and on Y." Or it can be "on both X and Y." Choice (C) has an invalid treatment of "both." So does (D). The correct answer is (E).

Fossilized remains of a horn thought to be of a triceratops found in sedimentary rock in 2011 <u>has been dated to be 65.5 million years old and thus is</u> evidence that dinosaurs existed shortly before the asteroid impact that is believed to have made them extinct.

- ○ has been dated to be 65.5 million years old and thus is
- ○ has been dated at 65.5 million years old and thus
- ○ have been dated to be 65.5 million years old and thus are
- ○ have been dated as being 65.5 million years old and thus
- ○ have been dated at 65.5 million years old and thus are

FOSSILIZED HORN

Fossilized remains of a horn thought to be of a triceratops found in sedimentary rock in 2011 <u>has been dated to be 65.5 million years old and thus is</u> evidence that dinosaurs existed shortly before the asteroid impact that is believed to have made them extinct.

- ○ has been dated to be 65.5 million years old and thus is
- ○ has been dated at 65.5 million years old and thus
- ○ have been dated to be 65.5 million years old and thus are
- ○ have been dated as being 65.5 million years old and thus
- ○ have been dated at 65.5 million years old and thus are

EXPLANATION

Creating a filter: in the original sentence, we can pause at "dated to be." That sounds funny. And if it doesn't sound funny to you, make a note of this specific idiom. We'll eliminate (A) and look for a replacement of "to be."

Applying the filter: in the other choices, the option "dated at" may sound funny as well. Perhaps we can evaluate the answer choices solely on other grounds.

Finding objective defects: all of the answer choices contain the word "thus," so that word won't be a factor. There are some verb differences at the end of the choices: "is," "are," and no verb. Omitting the verb at the end would create a sentence fragment. The grammatical subject of this verb, and the verb at the beginning of the underlined portion, is "remains," which is grammatically plural. "Horn" is a noun, but it's the object of the preposition "of," so it can't be the grammatical subject. That narrows our options to (C) and (E). We must decide between "to be" and "at." Indeed, in this question, we must know the idiom. The proper English idiom is "at." The correct answer is (E).

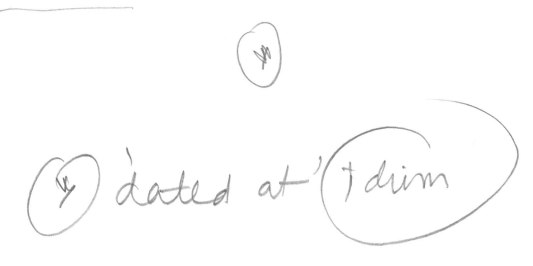

<u>Whereas in genetic mutation by insertion extra base pairs are inserted into the DNA, in mutation by substitution one base in the sequence is replaced for another.</u>

- Whereas in genetic mutation by insertion extra base pairs are inserted into the DNA, in mutation by substitution one base in the sequence is replaced for another.
- Whereas in genetic mutation by insertion extra base pairs are inserted into the DNA, mutation by substitution occurs when one base in the sequence is replaced for another.
- Unlike genetic mutation by insertion, where extra base pairs are inserted into the DNA, one base in the sequence is replaced for another in mutation by substitution.
- Unlike genetic mutation by insertion, where extra base pairs are inserted into the DNA, mutation by substitution replaces one base in the sequence with another.
- Unlike the case of extra base pairs inserted into the DNA, which is genetic mutation by insertion, in mutation by substitution one base in the sequence is replaced with another.

MUTATION BY SUBSTITUTION

Whereas in genetic mutation by insertion extra base pairs are inserted into the DNA, in mutation by substitution one base in the sequence is replaced for another.

- o Whereas in genetic mutation by insertion extra base pairs are inserted into the DNA, in mutation by substitution one base in the sequence is replaced for another.
- o Whereas in genetic mutation by insertion extra base pairs are inserted into the DNA, mutation by substitution occurs when one base in the sequence is replaced for another.
- o Unlike genetic mutation by insertion, where extra base pairs are inserted into the DNA, one base in the sequence is replaced for another in mutation by substitution.
- o Unlike genetic mutation by insertion, where extra base pairs are inserted into the DNA, mutation by substitution replaces one base in the sequence with another.
- o Unlike the case of extra base pairs inserted into the DNA, which is genetic mutation by insertion, in mutation by substitution one base in the sequence is replaced with another.

EXPLANATION

Creating a filter: supposing that we read the prompt and don't find any errors, we can proceed to choice (B) and come back to (A) later.

Finding objective defects: choice (B) is defective. The use of the word "when" is inaccurate here, because we are talking about *how* these mutations happen, not when. The comparison is also needlessly nonparallel. Choice (C) has a non-parallel comparison between "mutation by insertion" and "one base," so we eliminate choice (C). Choice (D) uses the word "where" incorrectly, because we aren't talking about location, and it attributes action to "mutation by substitution" rather than define the phenomenon. Choice (E) compares "case" with a non-case. The correct answer is (A).

A question for investors is whether there will be an end to the pattern according to which a social network attains an unprecedented number of <u>customers, which is dethroned by a new company with a slightly different product concept</u>.

- ○ customers, which is dethroned by a new company with a slightly different product concept
- ○ customers, then is dethroned by a new company with a slightly different product concept
- ○ customers but is dethroned by a new company with a slightly different product concept
- ○ customers, which is dethroned by a new company that has a slightly different product concept
- ○ customers and then is dethroned because a new company has a slightly different product concept

SOCIAL NETWORK THRONE

A question for investors is whether there will be an end to the pattern according to which a social network attains an unprecedented number of <u>customers, which is dethroned by a new company with a slightly different product concept</u>.

- ○ customers, which is dethroned by a new company with a slightly different product concept
- ○ customers, then is dethroned by a new company with a slightly different product concept
- ○ customers but is dethroned by a new company with a slightly different product concept
- ○ customers, which is dethroned by a new company that has a slightly different product concept
- ○ customers and then is dethroned because a new company has a slightly different product concept

EXPLANATION

Creating a filter: the original sentence has an error at the beginning of the underlined portion. As written, the clause "which is dethroned" modifies "customers," contrary to the intended meaning of the sentence. To keep it in reference to the about-to-be-dethroned social network, we must cut the comma from the phrase and add a conjunction, such as "and." We'll look for an answer choice that resolves this defect.

Applying the filter: answer choices (C) and (E) both roughly match what we are looking for. Choice (D) has the same problem as (A), and choice (B) creates a clause without a grammatical subject.

Finding objective defects: we are left with choices (C) and (E). Choice (E) draws us away from the intended meaning. "Dethrone" indicates that someone else is taking the throne, but (E) does not convey clearly that the new company is taking the throne. Also, the word "then" in (E) is inferior to the conjunction "but" in (C), because it fails to express the contrast between the two events in the pattern. The correct answer is (C).

Species that are colorful and aggressive in appearance <u>like, for example, the deadly coral snake are so numerous that in general predators are deterred as much by nonpoisonous imitation as by the true appearance of poisonousness</u>.

- o like, for example, the deadly coral snake are so numerous that in general predators are deterred as much by nonpoisonous imitation as by the true appearance of poisonousness
- o such as the deadly coral snake are so numerous that predators are deterred as much in general by nonpoisonous imitation as by the true appearance of poisonousness
- o such as the deadly coral snake are so numerous that in general predators are deterred as much by nonpoisonous imitation as the true appearance of poisonousness
- o like the deadly coral snake are so numerous that, in general, predators are deterred as much by nonpoisonous imitation as the true appearance of poisonousness
- o — for example, the deadly coral snake — are in general so numerous that predators are deterred as much by nonpoisonous imitation as the true appearance of poisonousness

POISONOUS COLORS

Species that are colorful and aggressive in appearance <u>like, for example, the deadly coral snake are so numerous that in general predators are deterred as much by nonpoisonous imitation as by the true appearance of poisonousness.</u>

- ○ like, for example, the deadly coral snake are so numerous that in general predators are deterred as much by nonpoisonous imitation as by the true appearance of poisonousness
- ○ such as the deadly coral snake are so numerous that predators are deterred as much in general by nonpoisonous imitation as by the true appearance of poisonousness
- ○ such as the deadly coral snake are so numerous that in general predators are deterred as much by nonpoisonous imitation as the true appearance of poisonousness
- ○ like the deadly coral snake are so numerous that, in general, predators are deterred as much by nonpoisonous imitation as the true appearance of poisonousness
- ○ — for example, the deadly coral snake — are in general so numerous that predators are deterred as much by nonpoisonous imitation as the true appearance of poisonousness

EXPLANATION

Creating a filter: we can pause early on in the original sentence, because the word "like" is redundant with the words "for example." So (A) is eliminated. In giving an example, "such as" is preferable to "like," since "like" is comparative in nature. We'll look for something like that.

Applying the filter: our expectation leads is to favor (B), (C), and (E).

Finding objective defects: choice (C) is missing the word "by" before "the true appearance"; the "by" is required because "as much... as" is a two-part construction requiring parallelism of its elements. In fact, (D) and (E) have the exact same problem. The correct answer is (B).

such as vs. like

North American cicadas always garner attention when they come above ground at the end of their 17-year life cycle, but in no case were they as well studied as <u>was their emergence during the 1920s</u>, when the naturalist William T. Davis studied them in detail.

- ○ was their emergence during the 1920s
- ○ had their 1920s emergence
- ○ in their emergence during the 1920s
- ○ their emergence during the 1920s was
- ○ their emergence during the 1920s

CICADA EMERGENCE

North American cicadas always garner attention when they come above ground at the end of their 17-year life cycle, but in no case were they as well studied as <u>was their emergence during the 1920s,</u> when the naturalist William T. Davis studied them in detail.

- ○ was their emergence during the 1920s
- ○ had their 1920s emergence
- ○ in their emergence during the 1920s
- ○ their emergence during the 1920s was
- ○ their emergence during the 1920s

EXPLANATION

Creating a filter: the original question contains a comparison. To examine this comparison more closely, we can ignore the first portion of the sentence; then we have, "In no case were they as well studied as..." Logically, the construction is like, "*X* was as well studied as *Y*," where *X* equals "in no case." *Y* could equal something like, "in this case," "in every other case," or "in the 1920s," but it must start with the preposition "in" to be parallel.

Applying the filter: The correct answer is (C).

According to a recent study, people may feel as refreshed upon waking from sleep of poor quality, as long as they believe they have slept well, <u>as from sleep of good quality</u>.

- ○ as from sleep of good quality
- ○ as after waking from good sleep
- ○ than from good sleep
- ○ as they feel from a good sleep
- ○ as upon waking from good sleep

SLEEP QUALITY

According to a recent study, people may feel as refreshed upon waking from sleep of poor quality, as long as they believe they have slept well, <u>as from sleep of good quality</u>.

- ○ as from sleep of good quality
- ○ as after waking from good sleep
- ○ than from good sleep
- ○ as they feel from a good sleep
- ○ as upon waking from good sleep

EXPLANATION

Creating a filter: the original sentences includes a distraction in the form of the modifying phrase, "as long as they believe they have slept well," which can be removed without affecting the surrounding grammar. What things are being compared? On one hand, "upon waking from sleep of poor quality." So the latter must be "upon waking from sleep of good quality." We'll look for that in the answer choices.

Applying the filter: none of the answers quite match our prediction (which is preferable to the answer choices), but the word "upon" is required for parallelism, regardless. The correct answer is (E).

WHAT'S NEXT?

Welcome to the end of the book! If you've worked through all of the practice questions in these pages, you are now familiar with the Sentence Correction questions you'll see on the GMAT.

Review these questions! It's worth reexamining every practice GMAT question at least twice. Further reviews help you view the question more strategically and ingrain in yourself the practices that you want to replicate when you sit for the test. And reviewing questions is especially important in Sentence Correction, because doing so allows you to absorb the idioms that tend to appear on GMAT questions.

- To practice other question types, see our online course, GMAT Free, at www.gmatfree.com.
- For more GMAT Prep resources, see our "GMAT Prep" page at www.gmatfree.com/gmat-prep/, which includes links to important resources such as GMATPrep, the software from the test maker.

Lastly, feel free to be in touch with us at www.gmatfree.com/contact-us/.

Good luck on the GMAT and in business school.

Andrew Mitchell
Chief Freedom Officer
GMAT Free, LLC

>> Download the free
SC Strategy Sheets
GMATFree.com/SC-Strategy-Sheets

INDEX OF QUESTIONS

Download the free SC Strategy Sheets at GMATFree.com/SC-Strategy-Sheets

 >> Download the free
SC Strategy Sheets

GMATFree.com/SC-Strategy-Sheets

Printed in Great Britain
by Amazon.co.uk, Ltd.,
Marston Gate.